LIGHT OF EMERSON

TWO THOUSAND QUOTABLE THOUGHTS AND EPIGRAMS

A Complete Digest with Key-Word Concordance

THE CREAM OF ALL HE WROTE

Majestic, Inspiring Thought-Provoking Paragraphs and Utterances of America's Greatest Literary Genius—the Most Quoted Man of Modern Times—Known as "The Sage of Concord"

By

Ralph Waldo Emerson

Compiled, Edited and Condensed into one volume by

H. H. Emmons

THE BOOK TREE
San Diego, California

Originally published
1930
The Rex Publishing Company
Cleveland, OH

New material, revisions and cover
© 2011
The Book Tree

ISBN 978-1-58509-344-1

Cover layout and design
Toni Villalas

Published by
The Book Tree
P O Box 16476
San Diego, CA 92176
www.thebooktree.com

GENERAL OUTLINE OF THE WORK

RALPH WALDO EMERSON, 1803-1882
American Scholar, Minister, Lecturer
Philosopher and Poet

INDEX TO ORIGINAL SUBJECTS

See Key-Word Concordance, pages 309 to 338

INDEX TO ORIGINAL SUBJECTS—*(Cont'd)*

INDEX TO ORIGINAL SUBJECTS—*(Cont'd)*

DEDICATION

TO THE MEMORY of the Author
of those Masterpieces of Literature
familiarly known as "The Essays",
and the Writer of various other inspiring Prose-Poems, but who frankly and
bravely said: "Thought is the property
of him who can adequately place it";
"as soon as we learn what to do with
borrowed thoughts they become our
own"; "thus all originality is relative
and every book a quotation"—Ralph
Waldo Emerson—this Work is respect-
fully dedicated.   H. H. E.

INTRODUCTION

SEVERAL years ago a literary critic and writer of Boston asked me to name three authors whose works, if allowed no others, I would select to take with me were I to spend the rest of my life alone on an isolated island. Without hesitation the first author named was Ralph Waldo Emerson and I have not as yet changed my opinion. Much of his writings is very inspiring and likely to be the most enduring of any and all time. Nearly every sentence contains a worthy thought and on almost every page may be found one or more literary gems of "purest ray serene". Books and their authors may come and go but, figuratively speaking, Emerson's words go on forever. The refined product of his fertile brain is too pure to tarnish with age, and much of his social and spiritual philosophy will shine on down through the ages as the brightest of fixed stars in the heavens of Truth. He appears as a literary Euclid and his utterances a simple "Revelation" of fundamental truths. He is our American Confucius. His Essays, Orations, Writings and Lectures gave us Intellectual Freedom and ushered in a New-Day Religion able to withstand the acid test of modern science, as all truths, whether spiritual or material, fit together.

A. Bronson Alcott says that Emerson's books "abound in strong sense, happy humor, keen criticism, subtle insight, noble morals, clothed in chaste and manly diction, fresh with the breath and health of progress." Oliver Wendell Holmes called his Harvard Oration on The American Scholar the "intellectual Declaration of Independence for America." Many writers and leaders of note, consciously or unconsciously, come under his influence. Ministers, teachers and public speakers of high standing scarcely ever make an important public address without resorting to Emerson. In the most popular Anthologies published he is quoted many more times than any other American. What an enviable position! The phrase "Emerson says" is constantly met with in cultured speech and classic English literature, illustrating the powerful and widespread influence of this modest New Englander. When the orator wants his words to be impressive he calls Emerson to his rescue. The reaction is instantly effective. Surely he is worthy of the title—"The Sage of Concord." Borrowing Ingersoll's striking figure on Shakespeare we may well say of Emerson that "he was an intellectual ocean whose waves touched all the shores of thought and from which now the isles and continents of thought receive their dew and rain." In a more credulous age he would probably have been sainted, notwithstanding such form of hero worship or deification would be the very opposite of Emersonian philosophy and an insult to his true culture. He belongs to that class of which he writes: "There is a class of men, individuals of which appear at long intervals, so eminently endowed with insight and virtue that they have been unanimously saluted as divine, and who seem to be an accumulation of that power we consider. Divine persons are character born, or, to borrow a phrase from Napoleon, they are victory organized."

While Emerson was an intellectual super-man, his ability, culture and character were largely the product of his ancestral influence. One biographer, George W. Cooke, says of him: "Eight generations of cultured, conscientious and practical ministers preceded him. In each generation they held the most advanced positions in religious thought." Therefore "we can better understand why there should be this fine bloom of thought" in his mind, and we can further understand "how native is the best of his culture. Such an ancestry, physical and spiritual, is a promise of the richest culture, and it is of the finest natural powers. Emerson not only made good this promise, but added to it a remarkable genius and a unique spiritual insight. To his ancestry he owes much of the quality and direction of that genius** and the rich spiritual grace of his thought. We may well propound his own question, 'How shall a man escape from his own ancestors?' "

Although it is very desirable to acquaint ourselves with this Thoroughbred's Complete Works it is plainly apparent that it is well nigh impossible to store in our minds all the great wealth of quotable expressions found in his writings, or to so intimately acquaint ourselves with his works as to easily apply or seek out his most pertinent saying for the particular occasion. Except for a limited number of his often quoted words we must rely on our own research and personal, painstaking notations, for many gems of thought, striking, virile passages, not generally quoted in Anthologies, are continually encountered throughout all of Emerson's writings. Many readers and students habitually make brief jottings and notations of such from the time they commence their study.

It seems therefore that a published compilation of substantially all of these striking, thought-provoking passages and paragraphs, even though sometimes debatable and seemingly far-fetched, culled and selected from all of Emerson's outstanding utterances and works, would fill a long-felt need for a condensed work of such a nature. Again, Robert Southey admonishes us: "If you would be pungent, be brief; for it is with words as with sunbeams: the more they are condensed, the deeper they burn." Hence the matter contained in this volume has been selected and arranged as a Digest, with a Key-word Concordance, in the hope and with the idea in mind that the ready accessibility of such a publication would naturally be conducive to practical use and a more general familiarity with Emerson's masterful expressions, high imaginings and ennobling ideals.

Grateful acknowledgment is hereby made of the valuable secretarial assistance rendered by my wife, Pauline T. Emmons, in the preparation of the manuscripts for this volume.

H. H. EMMONS.

Canton, Ohio,
Feb. 6th, 1930.

SELF-RELIANCE

A man should learn to detect and watch that gleam of light which flashes across his mind from within, more than the lustre of the firmament of bards and sages.   1

In every work of genius we recognize our own rejected thoughts; they come back to us with a certain alienated majesty. Great works of art have no more affecting lesson for us than this.   2

There is a time in every man's education when he arrives at the conviction that envy is ignorance; that imitation is suicide; that he must take himself for better or for worse as his portion; that though the wide universe is full of good, no kernel of nourishing corn can come to him but through his toil bestowed on that plot of ground which is given to him to till.   3

A man is relieved and gay when he has put his heart into his work and done his best.   4

Infancy conforms to nobody; all conform to it; so that one babe commonly makes four or five out of the adults who prattle and play to it.   5

Society is a joint-stock company, in which the members agree, for the better securing of his bread to each shareholder, to surrender the liberty and culture of the eater.   6

Whoso would be a man, must be a nonconformist.   7

I am ashamed to think how easily we capitulate to badges and names, to large societies and dead institutions.   8

Truth is handsomer than the affectation of love.   9

There is a class of persons to whom by all spiritual affinity I am bought and sold; for them I will go to prison if need be.
                                                                10

My life is for itself and not for a spectacle. I much prefer that it should be of a lower strain, so it be genuine and equal, than that it should be glittering and unsteady.   11

It is easy in the world to live after the world's opinion; it is easy in solitude to live after our own; but the great man is he who in the midst of the crowd keeps with perfect sweetness the independence of solitude.   12

A man must consider what a blind-man's-buff is this game of conformity.   13

For nonconformity the world whips you with its displeasure. And therefore a man must know how to estimate a sour face.   14

In your metaphysics you have denied personality to the Deity, yet when the devout motions of soul come, yield to them heart and life, though they should clothe God with shape and color.   15

With consistency a great soul has simply nothing to do. He may as well concern himself with his shadow on the wall. Speak what you think now in hard words and to-morrow speak what to-morrow thinks in hard words again, though it contradict every thing you said to-day.   16

Pythagoras was misunderstood, and Socrates, and Jesus, and Luther, and Copernicus, and Galileo, and Newton, and every pure and wise spirit that ever took flesh. To be great is to be misunderstood.   17

Men imagine that they communicate their virtue or vice only by overt actions, and do not see that virtue or vice emit a breath every moment.   18

The voyage of the best ship is a zigzag line of a hundred tacks. 19

Every true man is a cause, a country, and an age; requires infinite spaces and numbers and time fully to accomplish his design;—and posterity seem to follow his steps as a train of clients. 20

An institution is the lengthened shadow of one man. 21

All history resolves itself very easily into the biography of a few stout and earnest persons. 22

We lie in the lap of immense intelligence, which makes us receivers of its truth and organs of its activity. 23

The relations of the soul to the divine spirit are so pure that it is profane to seek to interpose helps. 24

All things are made sacred by relation to it,—one as much as another. All things are dissolved to their centre by their cause, and in the universal miracle petty and particular miracles disappear. If therefore a man claims to know and speak of God and carries you backward to the phraseology of some old mouldered nation in another country, in another world, believe him not. 25

The centuries are conspirators against the sanity and authority of the soul. Time and space are but physiological colors which the eye makes, but the soul is light; where it is, is day; where it was, is night. 26

We are like children who repeat by rote the sentences of grandames and tutors, and, as they grow older, of the men of talents and character they chance to see. 27

If we live truly, we shall see truly.   It is as easy for the strong man to be strong, as it is for the weak to be weak.

28

The soul raised over passion beholds identity and eternal causation, perceives the self-existence of Truth and Right, and calms itself with knowing that all things go well.   29

Nature suffers nothing to remain in her kingdoms which cannot help itself.   30

I like the silent church before the service begins, better than any preaching.   31

If you can love me for what I am, we shall be the happier. If you cannot, I will seek to deserve that you should.   32

If you are noble, I will love you; if you are not, I will not hurt you and myself by hypocritical attentions.   33

Prayer that craves a particular commodity, anything less than all good, is vicious.   34

But prayer as a means to effect a private end is meanness and theft.   It supposes dualism and not unity in nature and consciousness.   As soon as the man is at one with God, he will not beg.   35

Another sort of false prayers are our regrets.   Discontent is the want of self-reliance; it is infirmity of will.   Regret calamities if you can thereby help the sufferer; if not, attend your own work and already the evil begins to be repaired.   Our sympathy is just as base.   We come to them who weep foolishly and sit down and cry for company, instead of imparting to them truth and health in rough electric shocks, putting them once more in communication with their own reason.   The secret of fortune is joy in our hands.   Welcome evermore to gods and men is the self-helping man.   For him all doors are flung wide; him all tongues greet, all honors crown, all eyes follow with desire. Our love goes out to him and embraces him because he did not need it. We solicitously and apologetically caress and celebrate him because he held on his way and scorned our disapprobation. The gods love him because men hated him.   36

As men's prayers are a disease of the will, so are their creeds a disease of the intellect.   37

He who travels to be amused, or to get somewhat which he does not carry, travels away from himself, and grows old even in youth among old things.   38

Travelling is a fool's paradise. Our first journeys discover to us the indifference of places. At home I dream that at Naples, at Rome, I can be intoxicated with beauty and lose my sadness. I pack my trunk, embrace my friends, embark on the sea and at last wake up in Naples, and there beside me is the stern fact, the sad self, unrelenting, identical, that I fled from.
                                                                                                      39

The soul created the arts wherever they have flourished. It was in his own mind that the artist sought his model.
                                                                                                      40

Insist on yourself; never imitate.   41

That which each can do best, none but his Maker can teach him.   42

Shakespeare will never be made by the study of Shakespeare.
                                                                                                      43

Society is a wave. The wave moves onward, but the water of which it is composed does not.   44

Nothing can bring you peace but yourself. Nothing can bring you peace but the triumph of principles.   45

COMPENSATION

But men are better than their theology. Their daily life gives it the lie. Every ingenuous and aspiring soul leaves the doctrine behind him in his own experience, and all men feel sometimes the falsehood which they cannot demonstrate. For men are wiser than they know.   46

Every sweet hath its sour; every evil, its good. Every faculty which is a receiver of pleasure has an equal penalty put on its abuse. It is to answer for its moderation with its life. For every grain of wit there is a grain of folly. For everything you have missed, you have gained something else; and for every thing you gain, you lose something.   47

There is always some levelling circumstance that puts down the overbearing, the strong, the rich, the fortunate, substantially on the same ground with all others.   48

If the government is cruel, the governor's life is not safe. If you tax too high, the revenue will yield nothing. If you make the criminal code sanguinary, juries will not convict. If the law is too mild, private vengeance comes in.   49

Every occupation, trade, art, transaction, is a compend of the world and a correlative of every other. Each one is an entire emblem of human life; of its good and ill, its trials, its enemies, its course and its end. And each one must somehow accommodate the whole man and recite all his destiny.
50

The true doctrine of omnipresence is that God reappears with all his parts in every moss and cobweb.   51

Every secret is told, every crime is punished, every virtue rewarded, every wrong redressed, in silence and certainty.
52

The exclusive in fashionable life does not see that he excludes himself from enjoyment, in the attempt to appropriate it. The exclusionist in religion does not see that he shuts the door of heaven on himself, in striving to shut out others.

53

All infractions of love and equity in our social relations are speedily punished. They are punished by fear. Whilst I stand in simple relations to my fellow-man, I have no displeasure in meeting him. We meet as water meets water, or as two currents of air mix, with perfect diffusion and interpenetration of nature. But as soon as there is any departure from simplicity and attempt at halfness, or good for me that is not good for him, my neighbor feels the wrong; he shrinks from me as far as I have shrunk from him; his eyes no longer seek mine; there is war between us; there is hate in him and fear in me.   54

Benefit is the end of nature. But for every benefit which you receive, a tax is levied. He is great who confers the most benefits. He is base,—and that is the one base thing in the universe,—to receive favors and render none.   55

But because of the dual constitution of things, in labor as in life there can be no cheating. The thief steals from himself. The swindler swindles himself. For the real price of labor is knowledge and virtue, whereof wealth and credit are signs. These signs, like paper money, may be counterfeited or stolen, but that which they represent, namely, knowledge and virtue, cannot be counterfeited or stolen. These ends of labor cannot be answered but by real exertions of the mind, and in obedience to pure motives.   56

The law of nature is, Do the thing, and you shall have the power; but they who do not the thing have not the power.

57

The absolute balance of Give and Take, the doctrine that
every thing has its price,—and if that price is not paid, not
that thing but something else is obtained, and that it is impossible to get anything without its price,—is not less sublime
in the columns of a ledger than in the budgets of states, in the
laws of light and darkness, in all the action and reaction of
nature.   58

The league between virtue and nature engages all things to
assume a hostile front to vice.   The beautiful laws and substances of the world persecute and whip the traitor.   He finds
that things are arranged for truth and benefit, but there is no
den in the wide world to hide a rogue.   Commit a crime, and
the earth is made of glass.   Commit a crime, and it seems as if
a coat of snow fell on the ground, such as reveals in the woods
the track of every partridge and fox and squirrel and mole.
You cannot recall the spoken word, you cannot wipe out the
foot-track, you cannot draw up the ladder, so as to leave no
inlet or clew.   Some damning circumstance always transpires.
The laws and substances of nature,—water, snow, wind,
gravitation,—become penalties to the thief.
On the other hand the law holds with equal sureness for all
right action.   Love, and you shall be loved.   All love is mathe-
matically just, as much as the two sides of an algebraic
equation.   59

The good are befriended even by weakness and defect.   As
no man had ever a point of pride that was not injurious to him,
so no man had ever a defect that was not somewhere made use-
ful to him.   60

Every man in his lifetime needs to thank his faults.   As no
man thoroughly understands a truth until he has contended
against it, so no man has a thorough acquaintance with the
hindrances or talents of men until he has suffered from the one
and seen the triumph of the other over his own want of the
same.   Has he a defect of temper that unfits him to live in so-

ciety? Thereby he is driven to entertain himself alone and
acquire habits of self-help; and thus, like the wounded oyster,
he mends his shell with pearl.

Our strength grows out of our weakness.   61

A great man is always willing to be little. Whilst he sits
on the cushion of advantages, he goes to sleep. When he is
pushed, tormented, defeated, he has a chance to learn something; he has been put on his wits, on his manhood; he has
gained facts; learns his ignorance; is cured of the insanity of
conceit; has got moderation and real skill.   62

Blame is safer than praise. I hate to be defended in a newspaper. As long as all that is said is said against me, I feel a
certain assurance of success. But as soon as honeyed words of
praise are spoken for me I feel as one that lies unprotected before his enemies. In general, every evil to which we do not
succumb is a benefactor. As the Sandwich Islander believes that
the strength and valor of the enemy he kills passes into himself,
so we gain the strength of the temptation we resist.   63

There is a third silent party to all our bargains. The nature
and soul of things takes on itself the guaranty of the fulfilment
of every contract, so that honest service cannot come to loss.
                    64

The history of persecution is a history of endeavors to cheat
nature, to make water run up hill, to twist a rope of sand. It
makes no difference whether the actors be many or one, a tyrant
or a mob. A mob is a society of bodies voluntarily bereaving
themselves of reason and traversing its work. The mob is man
voluntarily descending to the nature of the beast. Its fit hour
of activity is night.   65

The martyr cannot be dishonored. Every lash inflicted is
a tongue of fame; every prison, a more illustrious abode; every
burned book or house enlightens the world; every suppressed

or expunged word reverberates through the earth from side to side.   Hours of sanity and consideration are always arriving to communities, as to individuals, when the truth is seen and the martyrs are justified.   66

There can be no excess to love, none to knowledge, none to beauty, when these attributes are considered in the purest sense. The soul refuses limits, and always affirms an Optimism, never a Pessimism.

Man's life is a progress, and not a station. His instinct is trust.   67

There is no tax on the good of virtue, for that is the incoming of God himself, or absolute existence, without any comparative.   Material good has its tax, and if it came without desert or sweat, has no root in me, and the next wind will blow it away.   68

If I feel over-shadowed and outdone by great neighbors, I can yet love; I can still receive; and he that loveth maketh his own the grandeur he loves.   Thereby I make the discovery that my brother is my guardian, acting for me with the friendliest designs, and the estate I so admired and envied is my own.   It is the nature of the soul to appropriate all things.   69

We cannot part with our friends.   We cannot let our angels go.   We do not see that they only go out that archangels may come in.   70

The death of a dear friend, wife, brother, lover, which seemed nothing but privation, somewhat later assumes the aspect of a guide or genius; for it commonly operates revolutions in our way of life, terminates an epoch of infancy or of youth which was waiting to be closed, breaks up a wonted occupation, or a household, or style of living, and allows the formation of new ones more friendly to the growth of character.
                                                                71

THE AMERICAN SCHOLAR

Is not indeed every man a student, and do not all things exist for the student's behoof?   72

There is never a beginning, there is never an end, to the inexplicable continuity of this web of God, but always circular power returning into itself.   Therein it resembles his own spirit, whose beginning, whose ending, he never can find,—so entire, so boundless.   73

Books are the best type of the influence of the past.   74

As no air-pump can by any means make a perfect vacuum, so neither can any artist entirely exclude the conventional, the local, the perishable from his book, or write a book of pure thought, that shall be as efficient, in all respects, to a remote posterity, as to contemporaries.   75

The sluggish and perverted mind of the multitude, slow to open to the incursions of Reason, having once so opened, having once received this book, stands upon it, and makes an outcry if it is disparaged.   76

Meek young men grow up in libraries, believing it their duty to accept the views which Cicero, which Locke, which Bacon, have given; forgetful that Cicero, Locke, and Bacon were only young men in libraries when they wrote these books.
                                                        77

Books are the best of things, well used; abused, among the worst.   78

I had better never see a book than to be warped by its attraction clean out of my own orbit, and made a satellite instead of a system.   79

Books are for the scholar's idle times. When he can read God directly, the hour is too precious to be wasted in other men's transcripts of their readings.   80

There is some awe mixed with the joy of our surprise, when this poet, who lived in some past world, two or three hundred years ago, says that (which lies close to my own soul.   81

When the mind is braced by labor and invention, the page of whatever book we read becomes luminous with manifold allusion. Every sentence is doubly significant, and the sense of our author is as broad as the world.   82

Action is with the scholar subordinate, but it is essential. Without it he is not yet man. Without it thought can never ripen into truth.   83

The world,—this shadow of the soul, or *other me*,—lies wide around. Its attractions are the keys which unlock my thoughts and make me acquainted with myself.   84

He who has put forth his total strength in fit actions has the richest return of wisdom.   85

I learn immediately from any speaker how much he has already lived, through the poverty or the splendor of his speech.   86

Character is higher than intellect. Thinking is the function. Living is the functionary. The stream retreats to its source. A great soul will be strong to live, as well as strong to think.   87

The office of the scholar is to cheer, to raise, and to guide men by showing them facts amidst appearances.   88

Success treads on every right step.   89

The world is his who can see through its pretension.   90

They (the poor and lowly) are content to be brushed like
flies from the path of a great person, so that justice shall be
done by him to that common nature which it is the dearest
desire of all to see enlarged and glorified.   They sun themselves in the great man's light, and feel it to be their own element.   They cast the dignity of man from their down-trod
selves upon the shoulders of a hero, and will perish to add one
drop of blood to make that great heart beat, those giant
sinews combat and conquer.   91

Each philosopher, each bard, each actor has only done for
me, as by a delegate, what one day I can do for myself.   92

Give me insight into to-day, and you may have the antique
and future worlds.   93

Man is surprised to find that things near are not less beautiful and wondrous than things remote.   94

The world is nothing, the man is all; in yourself is the law
of all nature, and you know not yet how a globule of sap
ascends; in yourself slumbers the whole of Reason; it is for you
to know all; it is for you to dare all.   95

CHARACTER

Those who listened to Lord Chatham felt that there was something finer in the man than anything which he said.

96

Character is centrality, the impossibility of being displaced or overset. A man should give us a sense of mass. Society is frivolous, and shreds its day into scraps, its conversation into ceremonies and escapes.

97

There is nothing real or useful that is not a seat of war.

98

We know who is benevolent, by quite other means than the amount of subscription to soup-societies.

99

Those who live to the future must always appear selfish to those who live to the present.

100

A word warm from the heart enriches me. I surrender at discretion. How death-cold is literary genius before this fire of life! These are the touches that reanimate my heavy soul and give it eyes to pierce the dark of nature.

101

There is a class of men, individuals of which appear at long intervals, so eminently endowed with insight and virtue that they have been unanimously saluted as *divine*, and who seem to be an accumulation of that power we consider. Divine persons are character born, or, to borrow a phrase from Napoleon, they are victory organized.

102

Every trait which the artist recorded in stone he had seen in life, and better than his copy.

103

Plato said it was impossible not to believe in the children of the gods, "though they should speak without probable or necessary arguments." I should think myself very unhappy in my associates if I could not credit the best things in history.

104

He who confronts the gods, without any misgiving, knows heaven; he who waits a hundred ages until a sage comes, without doubting, knows men. 105

I know nothing which life has to offer so satisfying as the profound good understanding which can subsist, after much exchange of good offices, between two virtuous men, each of whom is sure of himself and sure of his friend. It is a happiness which postpones all other gratifications, and makes politics, and commerce, and churches, cheap. For when men shall meet as they ought, each a benefactor, a shower of stars, clothed with thoughts, with deeds, with accomplishments, it should be the festival of nature which all things announce. 106

A divine person is the prophecy of the mind; a friend is the hope of the heart. 107

History has been mean; our nations have been mobs; we have never seen a man; that divine form we do not yet know, but only the dream and prophecy of such; we do not know the majestic manners which belong to him, which appease and exalt the beholder. 108

There are many eyes that can detect and honor the prudent and household virtues; there are many that can discern Genius on his starry track, though the mob is incapable; but when that love which is all-suffering, all-abstaining, all-aspiring, which has vowed to itself that it will be a wretch and also a fool in this world sooner than soil its white hands by any compliances, comes into our streets and houses,—only the pure and aspiring can know its face, and the only compliment they can pay it is to own it. 109

SPIRITUAL LAWS

The soul will not know either deformity or pain. If in the hours of clear reason we should speak the severest truth, we should say that we had never made a sacrifice. 110

Our young people are diseased with the theological problems of original sin, origin of evil, predestination and the like. These never presented a practical difficulty to any man,—never darkened across any man's road who did not go out of his way to seek them. These are the soul's mumps and measles and whooping-coughs, and those who have not caught them cannot describe their health or prescribe the cure. 111

What we do not call education is more precious than that which we call so. 112

We love characters in proportion as they are impulsive and spontaneous. The less a man thinks or knows about his virtues the better we like him. 113

Nature will not have us fret and fume. She does not like our benevolence or our learning much better than she likes our frauds and wars. 114

Love should make joy; but our benevolence is unhappy. Our Sunday-schools and churches and pauper-societies are yokes to the neck. We pain ourselves to please nobody. There are natural ways of arriving at the same ends at which these aim, but do not arrive. 115

It is natural and beautiful that childhood should inquire and maturity should teach; but it is time enough to answer questions when they are asked. Do not shut up the young people against their will in a pew and force the children to ask them questions for an hour against their will. 116

We judge of a man's wisdom by his hope, knowing that the perception of the inexhaustibleness of nature is an immortal youth.   117

God exists.   There is a soul at the centre of nature and over the will of every man, so that none of us can wrong the universe.   118

The whole course of things goes to teach us faith.   We need only obey.   There is guidance for each of us, and by lowly listening we shall hear the right word.   119

Place yourself in the middle of the stream of power and wisdom which animates all whom it floats, and you are without effort impelled to truth, to right and a perfect contentment.
                                                                 120

If we would not be mar-plots with our miserable interferences, the work, the society, letters, arts, science, religion of men would go on far better than now, and the heaven predicted from the beginning of the world, and still predicted from the bottom of the heart, would organize itself, as do now the rose and the air and the sun.   121

A man's ambition is exactly proportioned to his powers. The height of the pinnacle is determined by the breadth of the base.   Every man has this call of the power to do somewhat unique, and no man has any other call.   122

It is the vice of our public speaking that it has not abandonment.   Somewhere, not only every orator but every man should let out all the length of all the reins; should find or make a frank and hearty expression of what force and meaning is in him.   123

What we call obscure condition or vulgar society is that condition and society whose poetry is not yet written, but which you shall presently make as enviable and renowned as any.   124

A man is a method, a progressive arrangement; a selecting principle, gathering his like to him wherever he goes. He takes only his own out of the multiplicity that sweeps and circles round him.   125

What your heart thinks great, is great.   The soul's emphasis is always right.   126

It is vain to attempt to keep a secret from one who has a right to know it.   It will tell itself.   127

God screens us evermore from premature ideas.   128

There are graces in the demeanor of a polished and noble person 'which are lost upon the eye of a churl.   These are like the stars whose light has not yet reached us.   129

The scholar forgets himself and apes the customs and costumes of the man of the world to deserve the smile of beauty, and follows some giddy girl, not yet taught by religious passion to know the noble woman with all that is serene, oracular and beautiful in her soul.   Let him be great, and love shall follow him.   Nothing is more deeply punished than the neglect of the affinities by which alone society should be formed, and the insane levity of choosing associates by others' eyes.   130

There is no luck in literary reputation.   They who make up the final verdict upon every book are not the partial and noisy readers of the hour when it appears, but a court as of angels, a public not to be bribed, not to be entreated and not to be

overawed, decides upon every man's title to fame.   Only those
books comes down which deserve to last.   131

There are not in the world at any one time more than a
dozen persons who read and understand Plato,—never enough
to pay for an edition of his works; yet to every generation
these come duly down, for the sake of those few persons, as if
God brought them in his hand.   132

I have heard an experienced counsellor say that he never
feared the effect upon a jury of a lawyer who does not believe
in his heart that his client ought to have a verdict.   133

The world is full of judgment-days, and into every assembly
that a man enters, in every action he attempts, he is gauged
and stamped.   134

Never was a sincere word utterly lost. Never a magnanimity
fell to the ground, but there is some heart to greet and accept
it unexpectedly.   135

If you would not be known to do any thing, never do it.
A man may play the fool in the drifts of a desert, but every
grain of sand shall seem to see.   136

We know that the ancestor of every action is a thought.
                                                                 137

SPIRIT

The happiest man is he who learns from nature the lesson of worship. 138

The world is a divine dream, from which we may presently awake to the glories and certainties of day. Idealism is a hypothesis to account for nature by other principles than those of carpentry and chemistry. 139

As a plant upon the earth, so a man rests upon the bosom of God; he is nourished by unfailing fountains, and draws at his need inexhaustible power. Who can set bounds to the possibilities of man? Once inhale the upper air, being admitted to behold the absolute natures of Justice and Truth, and we learn that man has access to the entire mind of the Creator, is himself the creator in the finite. This view, which admonishes me where the sources of wisdom and power lie, * * carries upon its face the highest certificate of truth, because it animates me to create my own world through the purification of my soul. 140

We are as much strangers in nature as we are aliens from God. 141

PROSPECTS

Empirical science is apt to cloud the sight, and by the very knowledge of functions and processes to bereave the student of the manly contemplation of the whole.   142

There are far more excellent qualities in the student than preciseness and infallibility; that a guess is often more fruitful than an indisputable affirmation, and that a dream may let us deeper into the secret of nature than a hundred concerted experiments.   143

The ends of study and composition are best answered by announcing undiscovered regions of thought.   144

The problem of restoring to the world original and eternal beauty is solved by the redemption of the soul. The ruin or the blank that we see when we look at nature, is in our own eye.   145

There are innocent men who worship God after the tradition of their fathers, but their sense of duty has not yet extended to the use of all their faculties.   146

Is not prayer also a study of truth,—a sally of the soul into the unfound infinite? No man ever prayed heartily without learning something.   147

We make fables to hide the baldness of the fact and conform it, as we say, to the higher law of mind.   148

To the wise, therefore, a fact is true poetry, and the most beautiful of fables.   149

Every spirit builds itself a house, and beyond its house a world, and beyond its world a heaven. Know then that the world exists for you.   150

THE OVER-SOUL

As with events, so is it with thoughts. When I watch that flowing river, which, out of regions I see not, pours for a season its streams into me, I see that I am a pensioner; not a cause but a surprised spectator of this ethereal water; that I desire and look up and put myself in the attitude of reception, but from some alien energy the visions come.   151

If we consider what happens in conversation, in reveries, in remorse, in times of passion, in surprises, in the instructions of dreams, wherein often we see ourselves in masquerade,—the droll disguises only magnifying and enhancing a real element and forcing it on our distant notice,—we shall catch many hints that will broaden and lighten into knowledge of the secret of nature. All goes to show that the soul in man is not an organ, but animates and exercises all the organs; is not a function, like the power of memory, of calculation, of comparison, but uses these as hands and feet; is not a faculty, but a light; is not the intellect or the will, but the master of the intellect and the will; is the background of our being, in which they lie,—an immensity not possessed and that cannot be possessed.   152

What we commonly call man, the eating, drinking, planting, counting man, does not, as we know him, represent himself, but misrepresents himself. Him we do not respect, but the soul, whose organ he is, would he let it appear through his action, would make our knees bend. When it breathes through his intellect, it is genius; when it breathes through his will, it is virtue; when it flows through his affection, it is love. And the blindness of the intellect begins when it would be something of itself. The weakness of the will begins when the individual would be something of himself. All reform aims in some one particular to let the soul have its way through us; in other words, to engage us to obey.

Of this pure nature every man is at some time sensible. Language cannot paint it with his colors. It is too subtle. It is undefinable, unmeasurable; but we know that it pervades and contains us.   153

The soul requires purity, but purity is not it; requires justice, but justice is not that; requires beneficence, but is somewhat better; so that there is a kind of descent and accommodation felt when we leave speaking of moral nature to urge a virtue which it enjoins.   154

Speak to his heart, and the man becomes suddenly virtuous.
155

The action of the soul is oftener in that which is felt and left unsaid than in that which is said in any conversation. It broods over every society, and they unconsciously seek for it in each other. We know better than we do.   156

A certain tendency to insanity has always attended the opening of the religious sense in men, as if they had been "blasted with excess of light."   157

The soul is superior to its knowledge, wiser than any of its works. The great poet makes us feel our own wealth, and then we think less of his compositions.   158

Ineffable is the union of man and God in every act of the soul. The simplest person who in his integrity worships God, becomes God (Godlike).   159

So come I to live in thoughts and act with energies which are immortal. Thus revering the soul, and learning, as the ancient said, that "its beauty is immense," man will come to see that the world is the perennial miracle which the soul worketh, and be less astonished at particular wonders; he will learn that there is no profane history; that all history is sacred; that the universe is represented in an atom, in a moment of time. He will weave no longer a spotted life of shreds and patches, but he will live with a divine unity. He will cease from what is base and frivolous in his life and be content with all places and with any service he can render. He will calmly front the morrow in the negligency of that trust which carries God with it and so hath already the whole future in the bottom of the heart.   160

EXPERIENCE

Sleep lingers all our lifetime about our eyes, as night hovers all day in the boughs of the fir-tree.   161

In times when we thought ourselves indolent, we have afterwards discovered that much was accomplished and much was begun in us. All our days are so unprofitable while they pass, that 'tis wonderful where or when (we ever got anything of this which we call wisdom, poetry, virtue. We never got it on any dated calendar day.   162

Every ship is a romantic object, except that we sail in. Embark, and the romance quits our vessel and hangs on every other sail in the horizon. Our life looks trivial, and we shun to record it. Men seem to have learned of the horizon the art of perpetual retreating and reference.   163

I quote another man's saying; unluckily that other withdraws himself in the same way, and quotes me.   164

Every roof is agreeable to the eye until it is lifted; then we find tragedy and moaning women and hard-eyed husbands and deluges of lethe.   165

So much of our time is preparation, so much is routine, and so much retrospect, that the pith of each man's genius contracts itself to a very few hours.   166

There are moods in which we court suffering, in the hope that here at least we shall find reality, sharp peaks and edges of truth. But it turns out to be scene-painting and counterfeit. The only thing grief has taught me is to know how shallow it is.   167

[38]

Souls never touch their objects. An innavigable sea washes with silent waves between us and the things we aim at and converse with.   168

If to-morrow I should be informed of the bankruptcy of my principal debtors, the loss of my property would be a great inconvenience to me, perhaps, for many years; but it would leave me as it found me,—neither better nor worse.   169

Dream delivers us to dream, and there is no end to illusion. Life is a train of moods like a string of beads, and as we pass through them they prove to be many-colored lenses which paint the world their own hue, and each shows only what lies in its focus.   170

It depends on the mood of the man whether he shall see the sunset or the fine poem. There are always sunsets, and there is always genius; but only a few hours so serene that we can relish nature or criticism.   171

Of what use is genius, if the organ is too convex or too concave and cannot find a focal distance within the actual horizon of human life?   172

I knew a witty physician who found the creed in the biliary duct, and used to affirm that if there was disease in the liver, the man became a Calvinist, and if that organ was sound, he became a Unitarian.   173

Men resist the conclusion in the morning, but adopt it as the evening wears on, that temper prevails over everything of time, place and condition, and is inconsumable in the flames of religion.   174

Into every intelligence there is a door which is never closed, through which the creator passes.   175

I cannot recall any form of man who is not superfluous sometimes.   176

Divinity is behind our failures and follies also.   177

Intellectual tasting of life will not supersede muscular activity. If a man should consider the nicety of the passage of a piece of bread down his throat, he would starve.   178

A political orator wittily compared our party promises to western roads, which opened stately enough, with planted trees on either side to tempt the traveller, but soon became narrow and narrower and ended in a squirrel-track and ran up a tree. So does culture with us; it ends in headache.   179

We live amid surfaces, and the true art of life is to skate well on them.   180

Five minutes of to-day are worth as much to me as five minutes in the next millennium. Let us be poised, and wise, and our own, today.   181

We should not postpone and refer and wish, but do broad justice where we are, by whomsoever we deal with, accepting our actual companions and circumstances, however humble or odious, as the mystic officials to whom the universe has delegated its whole pleasure for us.   182

I am grown by sympathy a little eager and sentimental, but leave me alone and I should relish every hour and what it brought me, the potluck of the day, as heartily as the oldest gossip in the bar-room.   183

In the morning I awake and find the old world, wife, babes and mother, Concord and Boston, the dear old spiritual world and even the dear old devil not far off.   184

Life itself is a bubble and a skepticism, and a sleep within a sleep.   185

The wise through excess of wisdom is made a fool.   186

Life is a series of surprises, and would not be worth taking or keeping if it were not.   187

Every man is an impossibility until he is born; every thing impossible until we see a success.   188

But every insight from this realm of thought is felt as initial, and promises a sequel. I do not make it; I arrive there, and behold what was there already.   189

Most of life seems to be mere advertisement of faculty; information is given us not to sell ourselves cheap; that we are very great.   190

The spirit is not helpless or needful of mediate organs. It has plentiful powers and direct effects. I am explained without explaining, I am felt without acting, and where I am not.
190

It is very unhappy, but too late to be helped, the discovery we have made that we exist.   192

Nature and literature are subjective phenomena; every evil and every good thing is a shadow which we cast.   193

The universe is the bride of the soul. All private sympathy is partial.   194

No man at last believes that he can be lost, or that the crime in him is as black as in the felon. Because the intellect qualifies in our own case the moral judgments.   195

As I am, so I see; use what language we will, we can never say anything but what we are.   196

A sympathetic person is placed in the dilemma of a swim-
mer among drowning men, who all catch at him, and if he
give so much as a leg or a finger they will drown him.   197

Life wears to me a visionary face.   Hardest roughest action
is visionary also.   It is but a choice between soft and turbulent
dreams.   198

To know a little would be worth the expense of this world.
I hear always the law of Adrastia, "that every soul which had
acquired any truth, should be safe from harm until another
period."   199

I observe that in the history of mankind there is never a
solitary example of success,——taking their own tests of success.
                                                              200

In the solitude to which every man is always returning, he
has a sanity and revelations which in his passage into new
worlds he will carry with him.   201

MAN THE REFORMER

Every man should be open to ecstasy or a divine illumination, and his daily walk elevated by intercourse with the spiritual world.   202

The demon of reform has a secret door into the heart of every lawmaker, of every inhabitant of every city. The fact that a new thought and hope have dawned in your breast, should apprize you that in the same hour a new light broke in upon a thousand private hearts.   203

The general system of our trade (apart from the blacker traits, which, I hope, are exceptions denounced and unshared by all reputable men) is a system of selfishness; is not dictated by the high sentiments of human nature; is not measured by the exact law of reciprocity, much less by the sentiments of love and heroism, but is a system of distrust, of concealment, of superior keenness, not of giving but of taking advantage.
                                                                       204

I do not charge the merchant or the manufacturer. The sins of our trade belong to no class, to no individual. One plucks, one distributes, one eats. Every body partakes, every body confesses,—yet none feels himself accountable.   205

Suppose a man is so unhappy as to be born a saint, with keen perceptions but with the conscience and love of an angel, and he is to get his living in the world; he finds himself excluded from all lucrative works; he has no farm, and he cannot get one; for to earn money enough to buy one requires a sort of concentration toward money, which is the selling himself for a number of years, and to him the present hour is as sacred and inviolable as any future hour. Of course, whilst another man has no land, my title to mine, your title to yours, is at once vitiated.   206

We must have an antagonism in the tough world for all the variety of our spiritual faculties, or they will not be born. Manual labor is the study of the external world.   207

Why needs any man be rich? Why must he have horses, fine garments, handsome apartments, access to public houses and places of amusement? Only for want of thought. Give his mind a new image, and he flees into a solitary garden or garret to enjoy it, and is richer with that dream than the fee of a county could make him.   208

Can anything be so elegant as to have few wants and to serve them one's self?   209

What is a man born for but to be a Reformer, a Remaker of what man has made; a renouncer of lies; a restorer of truth and good, imitating that great Nature which embosoms us all, and which sleeps no moment on an old past, but every hour repairs herself, yielding us every morning a new day, and with every pulsation a new life?   210

Every great and commanding moment in the annals of the world is the triumph of some enthusiasm.   211

Our age and history, for these thousand years, has not been the history of kindness, but of selfishness. Our distrust is very expensive. The money we spend for courts and prisons is very ill laid out. We make, by distrust, the thief, and burglar, and incendiary, and by our court and jail we keep him so.   212

Let us understand that the equitable rule is, that no man should take more than his share, let him be ever so rich. Let me feel that I am to be a lover. I am to see to it that the world is the better for me, and to find my reward in the act.
          213

ADDRESS

(Before Senior Class, Divinity College, Cambridge)

A more secret, sweet, and overpowering beauty appears to man when his heart and mind open to the sentiment of virtue. Then he is instructed in what is above him.   214

The intuition of the moral sentiment is an insight of the perfection of the laws of the soul.   215

He who does a good deed is instantly ennobled. He who does a mean deed is by the action itself contracted. He who puts off impurity, thereby put on purity. If a man is at heart just, then in so far is he God.   216

Character is always known. Thefts never enrich; alms never impoverish; murder will speak out of stone walls.
            217

As we are, so we associate. The good, by affinity, seek the good; the vile, by affinity, the vile. Thus of their own volition, souls proceed into heaven, into hell.   218

In the sublimest flights of the soul, rectitude is never surmounted, love is never outgrown.   219

What these holy bards said, all sane-men found agreeable and true. And the unique impression of Jesus upon mankind, whose name is not so much written as ploughed into the history of this world, is proof of the subtle virtue of this infusion.
            220

Jesus Christ belonged to the true race of prophets. He saw with open eye the mystery of the soul. Drawn by its severe harmony, ravished with its beauty, he lived in it, and had his being there. Alone in all history he estimated the greatness of man.   221

That which shows God in me, fortifies me.   222

The divine bards are the friends of my virtue, of my intellect, of my strength. They admonish me that the gleams which flash across my mind are not mine, but God's; that they had the like, and were not disobedient to the heavenly vision.

223

The injustice of the vulgar tone of preaching is not less flagrant to Jesus than to the souls which it profanes.

224

Men have come to speak of the revelation as somewhat long ago given and done, as if God were dead.

225

It is very certain that it is the effect of conversation with the beauty of the soul, to beget a desire and need to impart to others the same knowledge and love. If utterance is denied, the thought lies like a burden on the man. Always the seer is a sayer. Somehow his dream is told, somehow he publishes it with solemn joy; sometimes with pencil on canvas, sometimes with chisel on stone, sometimes in towers and aisles of granite, his soul's worship is builded; sometimes in anthems of indefinite music; but clearest and most permanent, in words.

226

The spirit only can teach. Not any profane man, not any sensual, not any liar, not any slave can teach, but only he can give, who has; he only can create, who is. The man on whom the soul descends, through whom the soul speaks, alone can teach. Courage, piety, love, wisdom, can teach; and every man can open his door to these angels, and they shall bring him the gift of tongues.

227

It is time that this ill-supressed murmur of all thoughtful men against the famine of our churches;—this moaning of the heart because it is bereaved of the consolation, the hope, the grandeur that come alone out of the culture of the moral nature,—should be heard through the sleep of indolence, and over the din of routine.

228

Preaching is the expression of the moral sentiment in application to the duties of life. In how many churches, by how
many prophets, tell me, is man made sensible that he is an
infinite Soul; that the earth and heavens are passing into his
mind; that he is drinking forever the soul of God?   229

The test of the true faith, certainly, should be its power to
charm and command the soul, as the laws of nature control
the activity of the hands,—so commanding that we find pleasure and honor in obeying. The faith should blend with the
light of rising and of setting suns, with the flying cloud, the
singing bird, and the breath of flowers.   230

Whenever the pulpit is usurped by a formalist, then is the
worshipper defrauded and disconsolate.   231

There is poetic truth concealed in all the commonplaces of
prayer and of sermons, and though foolishly spoken, they may
be wisely heard.   232

The village blasphemer sees fear in the face, form, and gait
of the minister.   233

What life the public worship retains, it owes to the scat-
tered company of pious men, who minister here and there in
the churches, and who, sometimes accepting with too great
tenderness the tenet of the elders, have not accepted from others,
but from their own heart, the genuine impulses of virtue, and
so still command our love and awe, to the sanctity of character.
          234

But, with whatever exception, it is still true that tradition
characterizes the preaching of this country; that it comes out
of the memory, and not out of the soul; that it aims at what
is usual, and not at what is necessary and eternal; that thus
historical Christianity destroys the power of preaching, by
withdrawing it from the exploration of the moral nature of
man; where the sublime is, there are the resources of astonishment and power.   235

And what greater calamity can fall upon a nation than the loss of worship? Then all things go to decay. Genius leaves the temple to haunt the senate or the market. Literature becomes frivolous. Science is cold. The eye of youth is not lighted by the hope of other worlds, and age is without honor. Society lives to trifles, and when men die we do not mention them.
                                                    236

The assumption that the age of inspiration is past, that the Bible is closed; the fear of degrading the character of Jesus by representing him as a man;—indicate with sufficient clearness the falsehood of our theology. It is the office of a true teacher to show us that God is, not was; that He speaketh, not spake.
                                                    237

Imitation cannot go above its model. The imitator dooms himself to hopeless mediocrity.   238

We mark with light in the memory the few interviews we have had, in the dreary years of routine and of sin, with souls that made our souls wiser; that spoke what we thought; that told us what we knew; that gave us leave to be what we inly were.   239

The orators, the poets, the commanders encroach on us only as fair women do, by our allowance and homage.   240

You would compliment a coxcomb doing a good act, but you would not praise an angel.   241

Faith makes us, and not we it, and faith makes its own forms.   242

A whole popedom of forms, one pulsation of virtue can uplift and vivify.   243

Duty is one thing with Science, with Beauty, and with Joy.
                                                    244

NATURE

To go into solitude, a man needs to retire as much from his chamber as from society. I am not solitary whilst I read and write, though nobody is with me. But if a man would be alone, let him look at the stars. 245

There is a property in the horizon which no man has but he whose eye can integrate all the parts; that is, the poet. This is the best part of men's farms, yet to this their warranty-deeds give no title. 246

The lover of nature is he whose inward and outward senses are still truly adjusted to each other; who has retained the spirit of infancy even into the era of manhood. 247

In the woods is perpetual youth. Within these plantations of God, a decorum and sanctity reign, a perennial festival is dressed, and the guest sees not how he should tire of them in a thousand years. In the woods, we return to reason and faith. There I feel that nothing can befall me in life,—no disgrace, no calamity (leaving me my eyes), which nature cannot repair. * * I am the lover of uncontained and immortal beauty. In the wilderness, I find something more dear and connate than in streets and villages. 248

NATURE

(SECOND ESSAY)

At the gates of the forest, the surprised man of the world is forced to leave his city estimates of great and small, wise and foolish. The knapsack of custom falls off his back with the first step he takes into these precincts. Here is sanctity which shames our religions, and reality which discredits our heroes.
249

We nestle in nature, and draw our living as parasites from her roots and grains, and we receive glances from the heavenly bodies, which call us to solitude and foretell the remotest future.
250

The difference between landscape and landscape is small, but there is great difference in the beholders.
251

All changes pass without violence, by reason of the two cardinal conditions of boundless space and boundless time. Geology has initiated us into the secularity of nature, and taught us to disuse our dame-school measures.
252

Plants are the young of the world, vessels of health and vigor; but they grope ever upwards towards consciousness; the trees are imperfect men, and seem to bemoan their imprisonment, rooted in the ground. The animal is the novice and probationer of a more advanced order. The men, though young, having tasted the first drop from the cup of thought, are already dissipated; the maples and ferns are still uncorrupt; yet no doubt when they come to consciousness they too will curse and swear.
253

Every known fact in natural science was divined by the presentiment of somebody, before it was actually verified.
254

Nature sends no creature, no man into the world without adding a small excess of his proper quality. 255

The lover seeks in marriage his private felicity and perfection, with no prospective end; and nature hides in his happiness her own end, namely progeny, or the perpetuity of the race. 256

No man is quite sane; each has a vein of folly in his composition. 257

Remarkable is the overfaith of each man in the importance of what he has to do or say. The poet, the prophet, has a higher value for what he utters than any hearer, and therefore it gets spoken. 258

One may have impressive experience and yet may not know how to put his private fact into literature. 259

Our music, our poetry, our language itself are not satisfactions, but suggestions. 260

The accepted and betrothed lover has lost the wildest charm of his maiden in her acceptance of him. She was heaven whilst he pursued her as a star; she cannot be heaven if she stoops to such a one as he. 261

We are escorted on every hand through life by spiritual agents, and a beneficent purpose lies in wait for us. 262

THE METHOD OF NATURE

When Nature has work to be done, she creates a genius to do it. 263

A man's wisdom is to know that all ends are momentary, that the best end must be superseded by a better. 264

The poet must be a rhapsodist; his inspiration a sort of bright casualty; his will in it only the surrender of will to the Universal Power, which will not be seen face to face, but must be received and sympathetically known. 265

The imaginative faculty of the soul must be fed with objects immense and eternal. 266

When we speak truly,—is not he only unhappy who is not in love? his fancied freedom and self-rule—is it not so much death? 267

And the reason why all men honor love is because it looks up and not down; aspires and not despairs. 268

What a debt is ours to that old religion which, in the childhood of most of us, still dwelt like a sabbath morning in the country of New England, teaching privation, self-denial and sorrow! 269

Truth is always holy, holiness always wise. 270

The doctrine of this Supreme Presence is a cry of joy and exultation.*** I praise with wonder this great reality, which seems to drown all things in the deluge of its light. What man seeing this, can lose it from his thoughts, or entertain a meaner subject? The entrance of this into his mind seems to be the birth of man. We cannot describe the natural history of the soul, but we know that it is divine. I cannot tell if these wonderful qualities which house to-day in this mortal frame shall ever re-assemble in equal activity in a similar frame, or whether they have before had a natural history like that of this body you see before you; but this one thing I know, that these qualities did not now begin to exist, cannot be sick with my sickness, nor buried in any grave; but that they circulate through the Universe; before the world was, they were. Nothing can bar them out, or shut them in, but they penetrate the ocean and land, space and time, form an essence, and hold the key to universal nature.   271

Let those fear and those fawn who will. The soul is in her native realm, and it is wider than space, older than time, wide as hope, rich as love. Pusillanimity and fear she refuses with a beautiful scorn; they are not for her who puts on her coronation robes, and goes out through universal love to universal power.   272

CIRCLES

Our life is an apprenticeship to the truth that around every circle another can be drawn; that there is no end in nature, but every end is a beginning; that there is always another dawn risen on mid-noon, and under every deep a lower deep opens.

273

In the thought of to-morrow there is a power to upheave all thy creed, all the creeds, all the literatures of the nations, and marshal thee to a heaven which no epic dream has yet depicted. Every man is not so much a workman in the world as he is a suggestion of that which he should be. Men walk as prophecies of the next age. 274

Every man supposes himself not to be fully understood; ** that is, every man believes that he has a greater possibility.

275

A man's growth is seen in the successive choirs of his friends. For every friend whom he loses for truth, he gains a better.

276

Beware when the great God lets loose a thinker on this planet. Then all things are at risk. It is as when a conflagration has broken out in a great city, and no man knows what is safe, or where it will end. There is not a piece of science but its flank may be turned to-morrow; there is not any literary reputation, not the so-called eternal names of fame, that may not be revised and condemned. The very hopes of man, the thoughts of his heart, the religion of nations, the manners and morals of mankind are all at the mercy of a new generalization. Generalization is always a new influx of the divinity into the mind. Hence the thrill that attends it. 277

Valor consists in the power of self-recovery, so that a man cannot have his flank turned, cannot be out-generalled, but put him where you will, he stands. 278

Good as is discourse, silence is better, and shames it. The length of the discourse indicates the distance of thought betwixt the speaker and the hearer. If they were at a perfect understanding in any part, no words would be necessary thereon. If at one in all parts, no words would be suffered.   279

Cause and effect are two sides of one fact.   280

One man's justice is another's injustice; one man's beauty, another's ugliness; one man's wisdom, another's folly; as one beholds the same objects from a higher point.   281

If a man should dedicate himself to the payment of notes, would not this be injustice? Does he owe no debt but money? And are all claims on him to be postponed to a landlord's or a banker's?   282

There is no virtue which is final; all are initial. The virtues of society are vices of the saint. The terror of reform is the discovery that we must cast away our virtues, or what we have always esteemed such, into the same pit that has consumed our grosser vices.   283

But lest I should mislead any when I have my own head and obey my whims, let me remind the reader that I am only an experimenter. Do not set the least value on what I do, or the least discredit on what I do not, as if I pretended to settle any thing as true or false. I unsettle all things. No facts are to me sacred; none are profane; I simply experiment, an endless seeker with no Past at my back.   284

Nothing is secure but life, transition, the energizing spirit. No love can be bound by oath or covenant to secure it against a higher love. No truth so sublime but it may be trivial tomorrow in the light of new thoughts. People wish to be settled; only as far as they are unsettled is there any hope for them.
285

Nothing great was ever achieved without enthusiasm.   286

HISTORY

Every reform was once a private opinion.   287

There is properly no history, only biography.   288

To the poet, to the philosopher, to the saint, all things are friendly and sacred, all events profitable, all days holy, all men divine.   289

Every chemical substance, every plant, every animal in its growth, teaches the unity of cause, the variety of appearance.
290

Genius watches the monad through all his masks as he performs the metempsychosis of nature. Genius detects through the fly, through the caterpillar, through the grub, through the egg, the constant individual; through countless individuals the fixed species; through many species the genus; through all genera the steadfast type; through all the kingdoms of organized life the eternal unity. Nature is a mutable cloud which is always and never the same.   291

Nothing is so fleeting as form; yet never does it quite deny itself. In man we still trace the remains or hints of all that we esteem badges of servitude in the lower races; yet in him they enhance his nobleness and grace.   292

There is, at the surface, infinite variety of things; at the centre there is simplicity of cause.   293

Nature is an endless combination and repetition of a very few laws. She hums the old well-known air through innumerable variations.   294

It has been said that "common souls pay with what they do, nobler souls with that which they are."   295

Civil and natural history, the history of art and of literature, must be explained from individual history, or must remain words.** Strasburg Cathedral is a material counterpart of the soul of Erwin of Steinbach. The true poem is the poet's mind; the true ship is the ship-builder.   296

The whole of heraldry and of chivalry is in courtesy. A man of fine manners shall pronounce your name with all the ornament that titles of nobility could ever add.   297

The man who has seen the rising moon break out of the clouds at midnight, has been present like an archangel at the creation of light and of the world.   298

All public facts are to be individualized, all private facts are to be generalized. Then at once History becomes fluid and true, and Biography deep and sublime.   299

Every thing the individual sees without him corresponds to his states of mind, and every thing is in turn intelligible to him, as his onward thinking leads him into the truth to which that fact or series belongs.   300

Our admiration of the antique is not admiration of the old, but of the natural.   301

When a thought of Plato becomes a thought to me,—when a truth that fired the soul of Pindar fires mine, time is no more.   302

Rare, extravagant spirits come by us at intervals, who disclose to us new facts in nature. I see that men of God have from time to time walked among men and made their commission felt in the heart and soul of the commonest hearer.   303

Jesus astonishes and overpowers sensual people.   They cannot unite him to history, or reconcile him with themselves.
As they come to revere their intuitions and aspire to live holily,
their own piety explains every fact, every word.   304

A great licentiousness treads on the heels of a reformation.
How many times in the history of the world has the Luther
of the day had to lament the decay of piety in his own household.   305

When the gods come among men, they are not known.
Jesus was not; Socrates and Shakespeare were not.   306

Plato said that "poets utter great and wise things which they
do not themselves understand."   307

A man is a bundle of relations, a knot of roots, whose
flower and fruitage is the world.   His faculties refer to natures
out of him and predict the world he is to inhabit, as the fins
of the fish foreshow that water exists, or the wings of an eagle
in the egg presuppose air.   308

Who knows himself before he has been thrilled with indignation at an outrage, or has heard an eloquent tongue, or
has shared the throb of thousands in a national exultation or
alarm?   No man can antedate his experience, or guess what
faculty or feeling a new object shall unlock, any more than he
can draw to-day the face of a person whom he shall see to-
morrow for the first time.   309

But it is the fault of our rhetoric that we cannot strongly
state one fact without seeming to belie some other.   I hold our
actual knowledge very cheap.   310

I am ashamed to see what a shallow village tale our so-
called History is.   311

LECTURE ON THE TIMES
(1841)

Everything that is popular, it has been said, deserves the attention of the philopsopher; and this for the obvious reason, that although it may not be of any worth in itself, yet it characterizes the people.   312

As trees make scenery, and constitute the hospitality of the landscape, so persons are the world to persons.   313

There is no interest or institution so poor and withered, but if a new strong man could be born into it, he would immediately redeem and replace it.   314

We are the representatives of religion and intellect, and stand in the light of Ideas, whose rays stream through us to those younger and more in the dark.   315

A great deal of the profoundest thinking of antiquity, which had become as good as obsolete for us, is now re-appearing in extracts and allusions, and in twenty years will get all printed anew.   316

The world leaves no track in space, and the greatest action of man no mark in the vast idea.   317

I cannot find language of sufficient energy to convey my sense of the sacredness of private integrity. All men, all things, the state, the church, yea, the friends of the heart are phantasms and unreal beside the sanctuary of the heart.   318

The great majority of men, unable to judge of any principle until its light falls on a fact, are not aware of the evil that is around them until they see it in some gross form, as in a class of intemperate men, or slaveholders, or soldiers, or fraudulent persons.   319

Thinking, which was a rage, is become an art. The thinker gives me results, and never invites me to be present with him at his invocation of truth, and to enjoy with him its proceeding into his mind.   320

Every age has a thousand sides and signs and tendencies, and it is only when surveyed from inferior points of view that great varieties of character appear.   321

At the manifest risk of repeating what every other Age has thought of itself, we might say we think the Genius of this Age more philosophical than any other has been, righter in its aims, truer, with less fear, less fable, less mixture of any sort.
          322

Time is the child of the Eternity.   323

Let it not be recorded in our own memories that in this moment of the Eternity, when we who were named by our names flitted across the light, we were afraid of any fact, or disgraced the fair Day by a pusillanimous preference of our bread to our freedom.   324

All the newspapers, all the tongues of to-day will of course at first defame what is noble; but you who hold not of to-day, not of the times, but of the Everlasting, are to stand for it; and the highest compliment man ever receives from heaven is the sending to him its disguised and discredited angels.   325

LOVE

Every promise of the soul has innumerable fulfilments; each of its joys ripens into a new want. Nature, uncontainable, flowing, forelooking, in the first sentiment of kindness anticipates already a benevolence which shall lose all particular regards in its general light. The introduction to this felicity is in a private and tender relation of one to one, which is the enchantment of human life; which, like a certain divine rage and enthusiasm, seizes on man at one period and works a revolution in his mind and body; unites him to his race, pledges him to the domestic and civic relations, carries him with new sympathy into nature, enhances the power of the senses, opens the imagination, adds to his character heroic and sacred attributes, establishes marriage and gives permanence to human society.

326

All mankind love a lover. The earliest demonstrations of complacency and kindness are nature's most winning pictures. It is the dawn of civility and grace in the coarse and rustic.

327

But be our experience in particulars what it may, no man ever forgot the visitations of that power (love) to his heart and brain, which created all things anew; which was the dawn in him of music, poetry and art; which made the face of nature radiant with purple light, the morning and the night varied enchantments; when a single tone of one voice could make the heart bound, and the most trivial circumstance associated with one form is put in the amber of memory; when he became all eye when one was present, and all memory when one was gone; when the youth becomes a watcher of windows and studious of a glove, a veil, a ribbon, or the wheels of a carriage; when no place is too solitary and none too silent for him who has richer company and sweeter conversation in his new thoughts than any old friends, though best and purest, can give him; for the figures, the motions, the words of the beloved object are not, like other images, written in water, but, as Plutarch said, "enamelled in fire."

328

The passion (of love) rebuilds the world for the youth. It makes all things alive and significant. Nature grows conscious. Every bird on the boughs of the tree sings now to his heart and soul. The notes are almost articulate. The clouds have faces as he looks on them. The trees of the forest, the waving grass and the peeping flowers have grown intelligent; and he almost fears to trust them with the secret which they seem to invite.   329

It is a fact often observed, that men have written good verses under the inspiration of passion who cannot write well under any other circumstances.   330

It (love) expands the sentiment; it makes the clown gentle and gives the coward heart. Into the most pitiful and abject it will infuse a heart and courage to defy the world, so only it have the countenance of the beloved object.   331

The lover cannot paint his maiden to his fancy poor and solitary. ** Her existence makes the world rich.   332

The ancients called beauty the flowering of virtue.   333

The god or hero of the sculptor is always represented in a transition *from* that which is representable to the senses, *to* that which is not. Then first it ceases to be a stone. The same remark holds of painting. And of poetry the success is not attained when it lulls and satisfies, but when it astonishes and fires us with new endeavors after the unattainable.   334

Therefore the Deity sends the glory of youth before the soul, that it may avail itself of beautiful bodies as aids to its recollection of the celestial good and fair; and the man beholding such a person in the female sex runs to her and finds the highest joy in contemplating the form, movement and intelligence of this person, because it suggests to him the presence

of that which indeed is within the beauty, and the cause of the
beauty. 335

But this dream of love, though beautiful, is only one scene
in our play. In the procession of the soul from within outward, it enlarges its circles ever, like the pebble thrown into the
pond, or the light proceeding from an orb. 336

Thus are we put in training for a love which knows not
sex, nor person, nor partiality, but which seeks virtue and
wisdom everywhere, to the end of increasing virtue and wisdom.
We are by nature observers, and thereby learners. That is our
permanent state. But we are often made to feel that our affections are but tents of a night. Though slowly and with pain,
the objects of the affections change, as the objects of thought
do. There are moments when the affections rule and absorb
the man and make his happiness dependent on a person or
persons. But in health the mind is presently seen again,—its
overarching vault, bright with galaxies of immutable lights,
and the warm loves and fears, that swept over us as clouds,
must lose their finite character and blend with God, to attain
their own perfection. But we need not fear that we can lose
anything by the progress of the soul. The soul may be trusted
to the end. That which is so beautiful and attractive as these
relations, must be succeeded and supplanted only by what is
more beautiful, and so on forever. 337

FRIENDSHIP

We have a great deal more kindness than is ever spoken.
338

Friendship, like the immortality of the soul, is too good to be believed.
339

Almost all people descend to meet. All association must be a compromise, and, what is worst, the very flower and aroma of the flower of each of the beautiful natures disappears as they approach each other. What a perpetual disappointment is actual society, even of the virtuous and gifted!
340

Love, which is the essence of God, is not for levity, but for the total worth of man. Let us not have this childish luxury in our regards, but the austerest worth; let us approach our friend with an audacious trust in the truth of his heart, in the breadth, impossible to be overturned, of his foundations.
341

I do not wish to treat friendships daintily, but with roughest courage. When they are real, they are not glass threads or frostwork, but the solidest thing we know.
342

Every man alone is sincere. At the entrance of a second person, hypocrisy begins.
343

I hate the prostitution of the name of friendship to signify modish and worldly alliances. I much prefer the company of ploughboys and tin-peddlers to the silken and perfumed amity which celebrates its days of encounter by a frivolous display, by rides in a curricle and dinners at the best taverns.
344

Conversation is an evanescent relation,—no more. A man is reputed to have thought and eloquence; he cannot, for all

that, say a word to his cousin or his uncle. They accuse his silence with as much reason as they would blame the insignificance of a dial in the shade. In the sun it will mark the hour. Among those who enjoy his thought he will regain his tongue.
345

Better be a nettle in the side of your friend than his echo.
346

Friendship demands a religious treatment. We talk of choosing our friends, but friends are self-elected. Reverence is a great part of it.   347

The only reward of virtue is virtue; the only way to have a friend is to be one.   348

In the last analysis, love is only the reflection of a man's own worthiness from other men.   349

The higher the style we demand of friendship, of course the less easy to establish it with flesh and blood. We walk alone in the world. Friends such as we desire are dreams and fables. But a sublime hope cheers ever the faithful heart, that elsewhere, in other regions of the universal power souls are now acting, enduring and daring, which can love us and which we can love.   350

It never troubles the sun that some of his rays fall wide and vain into ungrateful space, and only a small part on the reflecting planet. Let your greatness educate the crude and cold companion.   351

It is thought a disgrace to love unrequited. But the great will see that true love cannot be unrequited.   352

THE POET

Men seem to have lost the perception of the instant dependence of form upon soul.   353

The highest minds of the world have never ceased to explore the double meaning, *** of every sensuous fact.   354

In love, in art, in avarice, in politics, in labor, in games, we study to utter our painful secret. The man is only half himself, the other half is his expression.   355

The great majority of men seem to be minors, who have not yet come into possession of their own.   356

For the Universe has three children, born at one time, which reappear under different names in every system of thought, whether they be called cause, operation and effect; or, more poetically, Jove, Pluto, Neptune; or, theologically, the Father, the Spirit and the Son; but which we will call here the Knower, the Doer and the Sayer. These stand respectively for the love of truth, for the love of good, and for the love of beauty.
357

Poetry was all written before time was, and whenever we are so finely organized that we can penetrate into that region where the air is music, we hear those primal warblings and attempt to write them down, but we lose ever and anon a word or a verse and substitute something of our own, and thus miswrite the poem.   358

Words and deeds are quite indifferent modes of the divine energy.   359

All that we call sacred history attests that the birth of a poet is the principal event in chronology.   360

Every line we can draw in the sand has expression; and there is no body without its spirit or genius. All form is an effect of character; all condition, of the quality of the life; all harmony, of health; and for this reason a perception of beauty should be sympathetic, or proper only to the good.   361

The Universe is the externization of the soul.   Wherever the life is, that bursts into appearance around it.   Our science is sensual, and therefore superficial.   The earth and the heavenly bodies, physics and chemistry, we sensually treat, as if they were self-existent; but these are the retinue of that Being we have.   362

Science always goes abreast with the just elevation of the man, keeping step 'with religion and metaphysics; or the state of science is an index of our self-knowledge.   363

The poorest experience is rich enough for all the purposes of expressing thought.   364

In the old mythology, mythologists observe, defects are ascribed to divine natures, as lameness to Vulcan, blindness to Cupid, and the like,—to signify exuberances.   365

The poet, by an ulterior intellectual perception, gives them a power which makes their old use forgotten, and puts eyes and a tongue into every dumb and inanimate object.   366

The poet alone knows astronomy, chemistry, vegetation and animation, for he does not stop at these facts, but employs them as signs.   He knows why the plain or meadow of space was strewn with these flowers we call suns and moons and stars; why the great deep is adorned with animals, with men, and gods; for in every word he speaks he rides on them as the horses of thought.   367

The etymologist finds the deadest word to have been once a brilliant picture.   Language is fossil poetry.   368

Genius is the activity which repairs the decays of things, whether wholly or partly of a material and finite kind.   369

A rhyme in one of our sonnets should not be less pleasing than the iterated nodes of a seashell, or the resembling difference of a group of flowers. The pairing of the birds is an idyl, not tedious as our idyls are; a tempest is a rough ode, without falsehood or rant; a summer, with its harvest sown, reaped and stored, is an epic song, subordinating how many admirably executed parts.   370

This insight, which expresses itself by what is called Imagination, is a very high sort of seeing, which does not come by study, but by the intellect being where and what it sees.
                                                                                      371

As the traveller who has lost his way throws his reins on his horse's neck and trusts to the instinct of the animal to find his road, so must we do with the divine animal who carries us through this world.   372

Bards love wine, narcotics and other procurers of animal exhilaration. ** All men avail themselves of conversation, music, pictures, sculpture, theatres, politics, love, gaming, or animal intoxication. ** These are auxiliaries to the centrifugal tendency of a man, to his passage out into free space, and they help him to escape the custody of that body in which he is pent up, and of that jail-yard of individual relations in which he is enclosed.   373

But never can any advantage be taken of nature by a trick. The spirit of the world, the great calm presence of the Creator, comes not forth to the sorceries of opium or of wine. The sublime vision comes to the pure and simple soul in a clean and chaste body. That is not an inspiration, which we owe to narcotics, but some counterfeit excitement and fury.   374

If thou fill thy brain with Boston and New York, with fashion and covetousness, and wilt stimulate thy jaded senses with wine and French coffee, thou shalt find no radiance of wisdom in the lonely waste of the pine woods.   375

I think nothing is of any value in books excepting the transcendental and extraordinary. If a man is inflamed and carried away by his thought, to that degree that he forgets the authors and the public and heeds only this one dream which holds him like an insanity, let me read his paper, and you may have all the arguments and histories and criticism. 376

On the brink of the waters of life and truth, we are miserably dying. The inaccessibleness of every thought but that we are in, is wonderful. What if you come near to it; you are as remote when you are nearest as when you are farthest. 377

Therefore all books of the imagination endure, all which ascend to that truth that the writer sees nature beneath him, and uses it as his exponent. Every verse or sentence possessing this virtue will take care of its own immortality. The religions of the world are the ejaculations of a few imaginative men. 378

The history of hierarchies seems to show that all religious error consisted in making the symbol too stark and solid, and was at last nothing but an excess of the organ of language. 379

We have yet had no genius in America, with tyrannous eye, which knew the value of our incomparable materials, and saw, in the barbarism and materialism of the times, another carnival of the same gods whose picture he so much admires in Homer. 380

Art is the path of the creator to his work. The paths or methods are ideal and eternal, though few men ever see them; not the artist himself for years, or for a lifetime, unless he come into the conditions. 381

THE CONSERVATIVE

It (conservatism) affirms because it holds. Its fingers clutch the fact, and it will not open its eyes to see a better fact. The castle which conservatism is set to defend is the actual state of things, good and bad. The project of innovation is the best possible state of things. 382

Conservatism stands on man's confessed limitations, reform on his indisputable infinitude; conservatism on circumstance, liberalism on power; one goes to make an adroit member of the social frame, the other to postpone all things to the man himself; conservatism is debonair and social, reform is individual and imperious. 383

Reform is affirmative, conservatism negative; conservatism goes for comfort, reform for truth. Conservatism is more candid to behold another's worth; reform more disposed to maintain and increase its own. Conservatism makes no poetry, breathes no prayer, has no invention; it is all memory. 384

Reform in its antagonism inclines to asinine resistance, to kick with hoofs; it runs to egotism and bloated self-conceit; it runs to a bodiless pretension, to unnatural refining and elevation which ends in hypocrisy and sensual reaction. 385

The leaves and a shell of soft wood are all that the vegetation of this summer has made; but the solid columnar stem, which lifts that bank of foliage into the air, to draw the eye and to cool us with its shade, is the gift and legacy of dead and buried years. 386

There is even no philosopher who is a philosopher at all times. 387

The existing world is not a dream, and cannot with impunity be treated as a dream; neither is it a disease; but it is the

ground on which you stand, it is the mother of whom you
were born.   388

Who put things on this false basis? No single man, but all
men. No man voluntarily and knowingly; but it is the result
of that degree of culture there is in the planet. The order of
things is as good as the character of the population permits.
                                                            389

The objection to conservatism, when embodied in a party,
is that in its love of acts it hates principles; it lives in the
senses, not in truth; it sacrifices to despair; it goes for available-
ness in its candidate, not for worth; and for expediency in its
measures, and not for the right.   390

Sickness gets organized as well as health, the vice as well as
the virtue. Now that a vicious system of trade has existed so
long, it has stereotyped itself in the human generation, and
misers are born. And now that sickness has got such a foot-
hold, leprosy has grown cunning, has got into the ballot-box;
the lepers outvote the clean; society has resolved itself into a
Hospital Committee, and all its laws are quarantine.   391

Religion among the low becomes low. As it loses its truth,
it loses credit with the sagacious.   392

If there be power in good intention, in fidelity, and in toil,
the north wind shall be purer, the stars in heaven shall glow
with a kindlier beam, that I have lived. I am primarily engaged to myself to be a public servant of all the gods, to demonstrate to all men that there is intelligence and good will at the
heart of things, and ever higher and yet higher leadings.   393

LITERARY ETHICS

Neither years nor books have yet availed to extirpate a prejudice then rooted in |me, that a scholar is the favorite of Heaven and earth, the excellency of his country, the happiest of men.   394

The scholar may lose himself in schools, in words, and become a pedant; but when he comprehends his duties he above all men is a realist, and converses with things.   395

The resources of the scholar are co-extensive with nature and truth, yet can never be his unless claimed by him with an equal greatness of mind. ** A divine pilgrim in nature (the scholar), all things attend his steps.   396

There is no event but sprung somewhere from the soul of man; and therefore there is none but the soul of man can interpret.   397

A false humility, a complaisance to reigning schools or to the wisdqm of antiquity, must not defraud me of supreme possession of this hour.   398

The youth, intoxicated with his admiration of a hero, fails to see that it is only a projection of his own soul which he admires.   399

Able men, in general, have good dispositions, and a respect for justice; because an able man is nothing else than a good, free, vascular organization, whereinto the universal spirit freely flows; so that his fund of justice is not only vast, but infinite.
                                                              400

Nothing is more simple than greatness; indeed, to be simple is to be great.   401

Truth is such a fly-away, such a slyboots, so untransportable and unbarrelable a commodity, that it is as hard to catch as light.   402

Think alone, and all places are friendly and sacred. The poets who have lived in cities have been hermits still. Inspiration makes solitude anywhere.   403

Out of love and hatred, out of earnings, and borrowings, and lendings, and losses; out of sickness and pain; out of wooing and worshipping; out of travelling, and voting, and watching, and caring; out of disgrace and contempt, comes our tuition in the serene and beautiful laws.   404

The vulgar call good fortune that which really is produced by the calculations of genius.   405

The man of genius should occupy the whole space between God, or pure mind, and the multitude of uneducated men. He must draw from the infinite Reason, on one side; he must penetrate into the heart and sense of the crowd, on the other. From one, he must draw his strength; to the other, he must owe his aim. The one yokes him to the real; the other, to the apparent. At one pole is Reason; at the other, Common Sense. If he be defective at either extreme of the scale, his philosophy will seem low and utilitarian, or it will appear too vague and indefinite for the uses of life.   406

If nevertheless God have called any of you to explore truth and beauty, be bold, be firm, be true. When you shall say, 'As others do, so will I; I renounce, I am sorry for it, my early visions; I must eat the good of the land and let learning and romantic expectations go, until a more convenient season;' ——then dies the man in you; then once more perish the buds of art, and poetry, and science, as they have died already in a thousand thousand men. The hour of that choice is the crisis of your history.   407

Be content with a little light, so it be your own.   408

BEAUTY

As the eye is the best composer, so light is the first of painters. There is no object so foul that intense light will not make it beautiful. 409

To the body and mind which have been cramped by noxious work or company, nature is medicinal and restores their tone. The tradesman, the attorney comes out of the din and craft of the street and sees the sky and the woods, and is a man again. In their eternal calm, he finds himself. 410

To the attentive eye, each moment of the year has its own beauty, and in the same field, it beholds, every hour, a picture which was never seen before, and which shall never be seen again. 411

Beauty is the mark God sets upon virtue. 412

When Sir Harry Vane was dragged up the Tower-hill, sitting on a sled, to suffer death as the champion of the English laws, one of the multitude cried out to him, "You never sate on so glorious a seat!" 413

Charles II *** caused the patriot Lord Russell to be drawn in an open coach through the principal streets of the city on his way to the scaffold. "But," his biographer says, "the multitude imagined they saw liberty and virtue sitting by his side." 414

An act of truth or heroism seems at once to draw to itself the sky as its temple, the sun as its candle. 415

The intellect searches out the absolute order of things as they stand in the mind of God, and without the colors of affection. 416

A work of art is an abstract or epitome of the world. It is the result or expression of nature, in miniature.   417

Nothing is quite beautiful alone; nothing but that which is beautiful in the whole.   418

No reason can be asked or given why the soul seeks beauty. Beauty, in its largest and profoundest sense, is one expression for the universe.   419

LANGUAGE

Every natural fact is a symbol of some spiritual fact. Every appearance in nature corresponds to some state of the mind.
                                                420

The corruption of man is followed by the corruption of language.   421

A Fact is the end or last issue of spirit. The visible creation is the terminus or the circumference of the invisible world.
                                                422

MANNERS

What fact more conspicuous in modern history than the creation of the gentleman? Chivalry is that, and loyalty is that, and in English literature half the drama, and all the novels, from Sir Philip Sidney to Sir Walter Scott, paint this figure. 423

Manners aim to facilitate life, to get rid of impediments and bring the man pure to energize. 424

The city is recruited from the country. In the year 1805. it is said, every legitimate monarch in Europe was imbecile. The city would have died out, rotted and exploded, long ago, but that it was reinforced from the fields. It is only country which came to town day before yesterday that is city and court to-day. 425

Fashion understands itself; good-breeding and personal superiority of whatever country readily fraternize with those of every other. 426

There is almost no kind of self-reliance, so it be sane and proportioned, which fashion does not occasionally adopt and give it the freedom of its saloons. 427

For there is nothing settled in manners, but the laws of behavior yield to the energy of the individual. The maiden at her first ball, the countryman at a city dinner, believes that there is a ritual according to which every act and compliment must be performed, or the failing party must be cast out of this presence. Later they learn that good sense and character make their own forms every moment, and speak or abstain, take wine or refuse it, stay or go, sit in a chair or sprawl with children on the floor, or stand on their head, or what else soever, in a new and original way; and that strong will is always in fashion, let who will be unfashionable. All that fashion demands is composure and self-content. 428

A man should not go where he cannot carry his whole sphere or society with him,—not bodily, the whole circle of

his friends, but atmospherically.   He should preserve in a new
company the same attitude of mind and reality of relation
which his daily associates draw him to, else he is shorn of his
best beams, and will be an orphan in the merriest club.   429

I would have a man enter his house through a hall filled with
heroic and sacred sculptures, that he might not want the hint
of tranquillity and self-poise.   We should meet each morning
as from foreign countries, and, spending the day together,
should depart at night, as into foreign countries.   In all things
I would have the island of man inviolate.   Let us sit apart as
the gods, talking from peak to peak all round Olympus.   430

Let us leave hurry to slaves.   431

Defect in manners is usually the defect of fine perceptions.
                                                             432

The love of beauty is mainly the love of measure or proportion.   433

One may be too punctual and too precise.   He must leave the
omniscience of business at the door, when he comes into the
palace of beauty.   Society loves creole natures, and sleepy lan-
guishing manners, so that they cover sense, grace and good-will;
the air of drowsy strength, which disarms criticism.   434

The line of heroes is not utterly extinct.   There is still ever
some admirable person in plain clothes, standing on the wharf,
who jumps in to rescue a drowning man.   435

A beautiful form is better than a beautiful face; a beautiful
behavior is better than a beautiful form; it gives a higher
pleasure than statues or pictures; it is the finest of the fine arts.
                                                             436

Everything that is called fashion and courtesy humbles itself
before the cause and fountain of honor, creator of titles and
dignities, namely the heart of love.   437

Without the rich heart, wealth is an ugly beggar.   438

DISCIPLINE

Nature is a discipline of the understanding in intellectual truths.   439

Debt, grinding debt, whose iron face the widow, the orphan, and the sons of genius fear and hate;—debt, which consumes so much time, which so cripples and disheartens a great spirit with cares that seem so base, is a preceptor whose lessons cannot be foregone, and is needed most by those who suffer from it most.   440

What good heed Nature forms in us! She pardons no mistakes. Her yea is yea, and her nay, nay.   441

The beauty of nature shines in his own breast. Man is greater that he can see this, and the universe less, because Time and Space relations vanish as laws are known.   442

Nothing in nature is exhausted in its first use. When a thing has served an end to the uttermost, it is wholly new for an ulterior service. In God, every end is converted into a new means.   443

All things with which we deal, preach to us. What is a farm but a mute gospel? The chaff and the wheat, weeds and plants, blight, rain, insects, sun,—it is a sacred emblem from the first furrow of spring to the last stack which the snow of winter overtakes in the fields.   444

Who can guess how much firmness the sea-beaten rock has taught the fisherman?   445

Xenophanes complained in his old age, that, look where he would, all things hastened back to Unity.   446

[78]

A leaf, a drop, a crystal, a moment of time, is related to the whole, and partakes of the perfection of the whole. Each particle is a microcosm, and faithfully renders the likeness of the world.   447

Each creature is only a modification of the other; the likeness in them is more than the difference, and their radical law is one and the same.   448

Words are finite organs of the infinite mind.   449

Words and actions are not the attributes of brute nature. They introduce us to the human form, of which all other organizations appear to be degradations.   450

IDEALISM

A noble doubt perpetually suggests itself,—whether this end be not the Final Cause of the Universe; and whether nature outwardly exists. 451

Any distrust of the permanence of laws would paralyze the faculties of man. 452

Nature is made to conspire with spirit to emancipate us. Certain mechanical changes, a small alteration in our local position, apprizes us of a dualism. 453

The Imagination may be defined to be the use which the Reason makes of the material world. 454

The true philosopher and the true poet are one; and a beauty, which is truth, and a truth, which is beauty, is the aim of both. 455

All men are capable of being raised by piety or by passion, into their region (Idealism). And no man touches these divine natures, without becoming, in some degree, himself divine. 456

Religion and ethics, which may be fitly called the practice of ideas, or the introduction of ideas into life, have an analogous effect with all lower culture, in degrading nature and suggesting its dependence on spirit. 457

The first and last lesson of religion is, "The things that are seen, are temporal; the things that are unseen, are eternal." 458
Culture inverts the vulgar views of nature, and brings the mind to call that apparent which it uses to call real, and that real which it uses to call visionary. 459

The soul sees something more important in Christianity than the scandals of ecclesiastical history or the niceties of criticism. 460

PRUDENCE

We write from aspiration and antagonism, as well as from experience. We paint those qualities which we do not possess. The poet admires the man of energy and tactics; the merchant breeds his son for the church or the bar; and where a man is not vain and egotistic you shall find what he has not by his praise.   461

Prudence is the virtue of the senses. It is the science of appearances. It is the outmost action of the inward life. It is God taking thought for oxen. It moves matter after the laws of matter. It is content to seek health of body by complying with physical conditions, and health of mind by the laws of the intellect.   462

The spurious prudence, making the senses final, is the god of sots and cowards, and is the subject of all comedy. It is nature's joke, and therefore literature's.   463

Do what we can, summer will have its flies; if we walk in the woods we must feed mosquitos; if we go a-fishing we must expect a wet coat.   464

The hard soil and four months of snow make the inhabitant of the northern temperate zone wiser and abler than his fellow who enjoys the fixed smile of the tropics. The islander may ramble all day at will. At night he may sleep on a mat under the moon, and wherever a wild date-tree grows, nature has, without a prayer even, spread a table for his morning meal.   465

Time is always bringing the occasions that disclose their value. Some wisdom comes out of every natural and innocent action.   466

The beautiful laws of time and space, once dislocated by our inaptitude, are holes and dens. If the hive be disturbed by rash and stupid hands, instead of honey it will yield us bees. Our words and actions to be fair must be timely.   467

Genius is always ascetic, and piety, and love. Appetite shows

[81]

to the finer souls as a disease, and they find beauty in rites and bounds that resist it.   468

The scholar shames us by his bifold life. Whilst something higher than prudence is active, he is admirable; when common sense is wanted, he is an encumbrance.   469

And who has not seen the tragedy of imprudent genius struggling for years with paltry pecuniary difficulties, at last sinking, chilled, exhausted and fruitless, like a giant slaughtered by pins?   470

In skating over thin ice our safety is in our speed.   471

Every violation of truth is not only a sort of suicide in the liar, but is a stab at the health of human society. On the most profitable lie the course of events presently lays a destructive tax; whilst frankness invites frankness, puts the parties on a convenient footing and makes their business a friendship. Trust men and they will be true to you; treat them greatly and they will show themselves great, though they make an exception in your favor to all their rules of trade.   472

He who wishes to walk in the most peaceful parts of life with any serenity must screw himself up to resolution. Let him front the object of his worst apprehension, and his stoutness will commonly make his fear groundless.   473

Every man is actually weak and apparently strong. To himself he seems weak; to others, formidable.   474

The natural motions of the soul are so much better than the voluntary ones that you will never do yourself justice in dispute.   475

Wisdom will never let us stand with any man or men on an unfriendly footing.   476

Life wastes itself whilst we are preparing to live.   477

Thus truth, frankness, courage, love, humility and all the virtues range themselves on the side of prudence, or the art of securing a present well-being.   478

INTELLECT

We do not determine what we will think. We only open our senses, clear away as we can all obstruction from the fact, and suffer the intellect to see. We have little control over our thoughts. We are the prisoners of ideas. 479

All our progress is an unfolding, like the vegetable bud. You have first an instinct, then an opinion, then a knowledge, as the plant has root, bud and fruit. Trust the instinct to the end, though you can render no reason. 480

What is the hardest task in the world? To think. 481

The ray of light passes invisible through space and only when it falls on an object is it seen. When the spiritual energy is directed on something outward, then it is a thought. The relation between it and you first makes you, the value of you, apparent to me. 482

God offers to every mind its choice between truth and repose. Take which you please,—you can never have both. Between these, as a pendulum, man oscillates. He in whom the love of repose predominates will accept the first creed, the first philosophy, the first political party he meets,—most likely his father's. He gets rest, commodity and reputation; but he shuts the door of truth. He in whom the love of truth predominates will keep himself aloof from all moorings, and afloat. He will abstain from dogmatism, and recognize all the opposite negations between which, as walls, his being is swung. He submits to the inconvenience of suspense and imperfect opinion, but he is a candidate for truth, as the other is not, and respects the highest law of his being. 483

The angels are so enamored of the language that is spoken in heaven that they will not distort their lips with the hissing and unmusical dialects of men, but speak their own, whether there be any who understand it or not. 484

ART

No man can quite emancipate himself from his age and country, or produce a model in which the education, the religion, the politics, usages and arts of his times shall have no share. 485

It is the habit of certain minds to give an all-excluding fulness to the object, the thought, the word they alight upon, and to make that for the time the deputy of the world. These are the artists, the orators, the leaders of society. The power to detach and to magnify by detaching is the essence of rhetoric in the hands of the orator and the poet. 486

Painting seems to be to the eye what dancing is to the limbs. 487

Though we travel the world over to find the beautiful, we must carry it with us, or we find it not. 488

Picture and sculpture are the celebrations and festivities of form. But true art is never fixed, but always flowing. 489

A great man is a new statue in every attitude and action. A beautiful woman is a picture which drives all beholders nobly mad. Life may be lyric or epic, as well as a poem or a romance. 490

As soon as beauty is sought, not from religion and love but for pleasure, it degrades the seeker. 491

THE YOUNG AMERICAN

It seems so easy for America to inspire and express the most expansive and humane spirit; newborn, free, healthful, strong, the land of the laborer, of the democrat, of the philanthropist, of the believer, of the saint, she should speak for the human race.   492

There is a sublime and friendly Destiny by which the human race is guided,—the race never dying, the individual never spared,—to results affecting masses and ages.   493

Nature is the noblest engineer, yet uses a grinding economy, working up all that is wasted today into tomorrow's creation; —not a superfluous grain of sand, for all the ostentation she makes of expense and public works.   494

Difference of opinion is the one crime which kings never forgive.   495

Trade, a plant which grows wherever there is peace, as soon as there is peace, and as long as there is peace.   496

The philosopher and lover of man have much harm to say of trade; but the historian will see that trade was the principle of Liberty; that trade planted America and destroyed Feudalism; that it makes peace and keeps peace, and it will abolish slavery.   497

Every line of history inspires a confidence that we shall not go far wrong; that things mend.   498

The whole value of the dime is in knowing what to do with it.   499

Money is of no value; it cannot spend itself. All depends on the skill of the spender. 500

We must have kings, and we must have nobles. Nature provides such in every society,—only let us have the real instead of the titular. 501

One thing is plain for all men of common sense and common conscience, that here, here in America, is the home of man. 502

It is one thing to visit the Pyramids, and another to wish to live there. 503

THE TRANSCENDENTALIST

Mind is the only reality, of which men and all other natures are better or worse reflectors. Nature, literature, history, are only subjective phenomena.   504

Everything real is self-existent.   Everything divine shares the self-existence of Deity.   All that you call the world is the shadow of that substance which you are, the perpetual creation of the powers of thought, of those that are dependent and of those that are independent of your will.   505

We have had many harbingers and forerunners; but of a purely spiritual life, history has afforded no example.   I mean we have yet no man who has leaned entirely on his character, and eaten angels' food; who, trusting to his sentiments, found life made of miracles; who, working for universal aims, found himself fed, he knew not how; clothed, sheltered, and weaponed, he knew not how, and yet it was done by his own hands.   506

Society, to be sure, does not like this very well; it saith, Whoso goes to walk alone, accuses the whole world; he declares all to be unfit to be his companions; it is very uncivil, nay, insulting; Society will retaliate.   507

Every moment of a hero so raises and cheers us that a twelve-month is an age.   508

It is the quality of the moment, not the number of days, of events, or of actors, that imports.   509

Much of our reading, much of our labor, seems mere waiting; it was not that we were born for.   510

When we pass, as presently we shall, into some new infinitude, out of this Iceland of negations, it will please us to reflect that though we had few virtues or consolations, we bore with our indigence, nor once strove to repair it with hypocrisy.
511

Amidst the downward tendency and proneness of things, when every voice is raised for a new road or another statute or a subscription of stock; for an improvement in dress, or in dentistry; for a new house or a larger business; for a political party, or the division of an estate;—will you not tolerate one or two solitary voices in the land, speaking for thoughts and principles not marketable or perishable?   Soon these improvements and mechanical inventions will be superseded; these modes of living lost out of memory; these cities rotted, ruined by war, by new inventions, by new seats of trade, or the geologic changes;—all gone, like the shells which sprinkle the sea-beach with a white colony today, forever renewed to be forever destroyed.   But the thoughts which these few hermits strove to proclaim by silence as well as by speech, not only by what they did, but by what they forbore to do, shall abide in beauty and strength, to reorganize themselves in nature, to invest themselves anew in other, perhaps higher endowed and happier mixed clay than ours, in fuller union with the surrounding system.
512

POLITICS

The wise know that foolish legislation is a rope of sand which perishes in the twisting.   513

The history of the State sketches in coarse outline the progress of thought, and follows at a distance the delicacy of culture and of aspiration.   514

The only interest for the consideration of the State is persons; that property will always follow persons; that the highest end of government is the culture of men; and that if men can be educated, the institutions will share their improvement and the moral sentiment will write the law of the land.   515

The spirit of our American radicalism is destructive and aimless; it is not loving; it has no ulterior and divine ends, but is destructive only out of hatred and selfishness.   On the other side, the conservative party, composed of the most moderate, able and cultivated part of the population, is timid, and merely defensive of property.   It vindicates no right, it aspires to no real good, it brands no crime, it proposes no generous policy; it does not build, nor write, nor cherish the arts, nor foster religion, nor establish schools, nor encourage science.   (1844).
516

Wild liberty develops iron conscience.   Want of liberty, by strengthening law and decorum, stupefies conscience.   "Lynch-law" prevails only where there is greater hardihood and self-subsistency in the leaders.   A mob cannot be a permanency; everybody's interest requires that it should not exist, and only justice satisfies all.   517

Every man finds a sanction for his simplest claims and deeds, in decisions of his own mind, which he calls Truth and Holiness.   518

All forms of government symbolize an immortal government, common to all dynasties and independent of numbers, perfect where two men exist, perfect where there is only one man.   519

Every man's nature is a sufficient advertisement to him of the character of his fellows.   520

The less government we have the better,—the fewer laws, and the less confided power.   521

We think our civilization near its meridian, but we are yet only at the cock-crowing and the morning star. In our barbarous society the influence of character is in its infancy.   522

Most persons of ability meet in society with a kind of tacit appeal. Each seems to say, "I am not all here." Senators and presidents have climbed so high with pain enough, not because they think the place specially agreeable, but as an apology for real worth, and to vindicate their manhood in our eyes.   523

What is strange too, there never was in any man sufficient faith in the power of rectitude to inspire him with the broad design of renovating the State on the principle of right and love.   524

GIFTS

Flowers and fruits are always fit presents;. flowers, because
they are a proud assertion that a ray of beauty outvalues all
the utilities of the world.   525

We love flattery even though we are not deceived by it, because it shows that we are of importance enough to be courted.
                                                               526

Necessity does everything well.   527

It is a cold lifeless business when you go to the shops to
buy me something which does not represent your life and talent,
but a goldsmith's.   528

We do not quite forgive a giver. The hand that feeds us
is in some danger of being bitten. We can receive anything
from love, for that is a way of receiving it from ourselves; but
not from any one who assumes to bestow. We sometimes hate
the meat which we eat, because there seems something of degrading dependence in living by it.   529

We arraign society if it do not give us, besides earth and
fire and water, opportunity, love, reverence and objects of
veneration.   530

He is a good man who can receive a gift well. We are either
glad or sorry at a gift, and both emotions are unbecoming.
                                                               531

It is a great happiness to get off without injury and heart-
burning from one who has had the ill-luck to be served by
you.   532

You cannot give anything to a magnanimous person. After you have served him he at once puts you in debt by his magnanimity.   533

I fear to breathe any treason against the majesty of love, which is the genius and god of gifts, and to whom we must not affect to prescribe.   534

HEROISM

We need books of this tart cathartic virtue more than books of political science or of private economy. 535

To this military attitude of the soul we give the name of Heroism. 536

Heroism is an obedience to a secret impulse of an individual's character. 537

Self-trust is the essence of heroism. It is the state of the soul at war, and its ultimate objects are the last defiance of falsehood and wrong, and the power to bear all that can be inflicted by evil agents. It speaks the truth and it is just, generous, hospitable, temperate, scornful of petty calculations and scornful of being scorned. 538

That false prudence which dotes on health and wealth is the butt and merriment of heroism. Heroism, like Plotinus, is almost ashamed of its body. 539

A great man scarcely knows how he dines, how he dresses; but without railing or precision his living is natural and poetic. 540

The great will not condescend to take any thing seriously; all must be as gay as the song of a canary, though it were the building of cities or the eradication of old and foolish churches and nations which have cumbered the earth long thousands of years. 541

A great man makes his climate genial in the imagination of men, and its air the beloved element of all delicate spirits. That

country is the fairest which is inhabited by the noblest minds.
542

Times of heroism are generally times of terror, but the day never shines in which this element may not work.   543

Who that sees the meanness of our politics but inly congratulates Washington that he is long already wrapped in his shroud, and for ever safe; that he was laid sweet in his grave, the hope of humanity not yet subjugated in him? Who does not sometimes envy the good and brave who are no more to suffer from the tumults of the natural world, and await with curious complacency the speedy term of his own conversation with finite nature?   544

USES OF GREAT MEN

Nature seems to exist for the excellent. The world is upheld by the veracity of good men; they make the earth wholesome. 545

The search after the great man is the dream of youth and the most serious occupation of manhood. 546

Other men are lenses through which we read our own minds. 547

I count him a great man who inhabits a higher sphere of thought, into which other men rise with labor and difficulty. 548

He is great who is what he is from nature, and who never reminds us of others. 549

Right ethics are central and go from the soul outward. Gift is contrary to the law of the universe. Serving others is serving us. 550

Each plant has its parasite, and each created thing its lover and poet. 551

Each material thing has its celestial side; has its translation, through humanity, into the spiritual and necessary sphere where it plays a part as indestructible as any other. And to these, their ends, all things continually ascend. The gases gather to the solid firmament; the chemic lump arrives at the plant, and grows; arrives at the quadruped, and walks; arrives at the man, and thinks. 552

Man, made of the dust of the world, does not forget his

origin; and all that is yet inanimate will one day speak and reason.　　　　　　　　　　　　　　　　　　　　　　　　　　553

Talk much with any man of vigorous mind, and we acquire
very fast the habit of looking at things in the same light.　554

There is a power in love to divine another's destiny better
than that other can, and, by heroic encouragements, hold him
to his task.　　　　　　　　　　　　　　　　　　　　　555

Shakespeare's principal merit may be conveyed in saying that
he of all men best understands the English language, and can
say what he will.　　　　　　　　　　　　　　　　　556

We are as elastic as the gas of gunpowder, and a sentence in
a book, or a word dropped in conversation, sets free our fancy,
and instantly our heads are bathed with galaxies, and our feet
tread the floor of the Pit.　　　　　　　　　　　　　557

The imbecility of men is always inviting the impudence of
power. It is the delight of vulgar talent to dazzle and to blind
the beholder. But true genius seeks to defend us from itself.
　　　　　　　　　　　　　　　　　　　　　　　　　558

Nobody is glad in the gladness of another, and our system
is one of war, of an injurious superiority. Every child of the
Saxon race is educated to wish to be first. It is our system;
and a man comes to measure his greatness by the regrets, envies
and hatreds of his competitors.　　　　　　　　　　　559

The worthless and offensive members of society, whose existence is a social pest, invariably think themselves the most
ill-used people alive, and never get over their astonishment at
the ingratitude and selfishness of their contemporaries.　560

It is very easy to be as wise and good as your companions.
561

Every mother wishes one son a genius, though all the rest should be mediocre.   562

Men who know the same things are not long the best company for each other.   563

As to what we call the masses, and common men,—there are no common men.   564

The reputations of the nineteenth century will one day be quoted to prove its barbarism. The genius of humanity is the real subject whose biography is written in our annals. We must infer much, and supply many chasms in the record. 565

The genius of humanity is the right point of view of history.   566

For a time our teachers serve us personally, as metres or milestones of progress. Once they were angels of knowledge and their figures touched the sky. Then we drew near, saw their means, culture and limits; and they yielded their places to other geniuses.   567

NOMINALIST AND REALIST

Great men or men of great gifts you shall easily find, but symmetrical men never. 568

Our exaggeration of all fine characters arises from the fact that we identify each in turn with the soul. But there are no such men as we fable. 569

It is bad enough that our geniuses cannot do anything useful, but it is worse that no man is fit for society who has fine traits. He is admired at a distance, but he cannot come near without appearing a cripple. 570

The magnetism which arranges tribes and races in one polarity is alone to be respected; the men are steel-filings. 571

A personal influence is an *ignis fatuus*. If they say it is great, it is great; if they say it is small, it is small; you see it, and you see it not, by turns; it borrows all its size from the momentary estimation of the speakers; the Will-of-the-wisp vanishes if you go too near, vanishes if you go too far. 572

Money, which represents the prose of life, and which is hardly spoken of in parlors without an apology, is, in its effects and laws, as beautiful as roses. 573

The modernness of all good books seems to give me an existence as wide as man. 574

I find the most pleasure in reading a book in a manner least flattering to the author. 575

It is a greater joy to see the author's author, than himself. 576

This preference of the genius to the parts is the secret of that deification of art, which is found in all superior minds.   577

The sanity of society is a balance of a thousand insanities. She punishes abstractionists, and will only forgive an induction which is rare and casual.   578

Each man too is a tyrant in tendency, because he would impose his idea on others; and their trick is their natural defence. Jesus would absorb the race; but Tom Paine or the coarsest blasphemer helps humanity by resisting this exuberance of power.   579

For rightly every man is a channel through which heaven floweth.   580

It is the secret of the world that all things subsist and do not die, but only retire a little from sight and afterwards return again.   581

NEW ENGLAND REFORMERS

The sight of a planet through a telescope is worth all the course on astronomy; the shock of the electric spark in the elbow, outvalues all the theories; the taste of the nitrous oxide, the firing of an artificial volcano, are better than volumes of chemistry.   582

But in a hundred high schools and colleges this warfare against common-sense still goes on. Four, or six, or ten years, the pupil is parsing Greek and Latin, and as soon as he leaves the University, as it is ludicrously styled, he shuts those books for the last time. Some thousands of young men are graduated at our colleges in this country every year, and the persons who, at forty years, still read Greek, can all be counted on your hand. I never met with ten. Four or five persons I have seen who read Plato.

But is not this absurd, that the whole liberal talent of this country should be directed in its best years on studies which lead to nothing?   583

Society gains nothing whilst a man, not himself renovated, attempts to renovate things around him; he has become tediously good in some particular but negligent or narrow in the rest; and hypocrisy and vanity are often the disgusting result.
                                                                584

If I should go out of church whenever I heard a false sentiment I could never stay there five minutes. But why come out? the street is as false as the church.   585

The soul lets no man go without some visitations and holy-days of a diviner presence.   586

What is it men love in Genius, but its infinite hope, which degrades all it has done? Genius counts all its miracles poor and short. Its own idea it never executed.   587

Men are conservatives when they are least vigorous, or when they are most luxurious. They are conservatives after dinner, or before taking their rest; when they are sick, or aged. In the morning, or when their intellect or their conscience has been aroused; when they hear music, or when they read poetry, they are radicals. 588

The selfish man suffers more from his selfishness than he from whom that selfishness withholds some important benefit. 589

Nothing shall warp me from the belief that every man is a lover of truth. There is no pure lie, no pure malignity in nature. The entertainment of the proposition of depravity is the last profligacy and profanation. There is no scepticism, no atheism but that. Could it be received into common belief, suicide would unpeople the planet. 590

A few years ago, the liberal churches complained that the Calvinistic church denied to them the name of Christian. I think the complaint was confession; a religious church would not complain. 591

The life of man is the true romance, which when it is valiantly conducted will yield the imagination a higher joy than any fiction. 592

It is so wonderful to our neurologists that a man can see without his eyes, that it does not occur to them that it is just as wonderful that he should see with them. 593

PLATO; OR, THE PHILOSOPHER

(427-347, B. C.)

Plato is philosophy, and philosophy, Plato,—at once the glory and the shame of mankind, since neither Saxon nor Roman have availed to add any idea to his categories.   594

Every book is a quotation; and every house is a quotation out of all forests and mines and stone quarries; and every man is a quotation from all his ancestors.   595

Great geniuses have the shortest biographies.   Their cousins can tell you nothing about them.   They lived in their writings, and so their house and street life was trivial and commonplace.   596

If the tongue had not been framed for articulation, man would still be a beast in the forest.   597

Philosophy is the account which the human mind gives to itself of the constitution of the world.   598

Socrates and Plato are the double star which the most powerful instruments will not entirely separate.   599

PLATO: SECOND ESSAY

The mind does not create what it perceives, any more than the eye creates the rose.   600

Plato affirms the coincidence of science and virtue; for vice can never know itself and virtue, but virtue knows itself and vice.   601

MONTAIGNE; OR, THE SKEPTIC

(1533-1592)

Every fact is related on one side to sensation, and on the other to morals. 602

The literary class is usually proud and exclusive. 603

No man acquires property without acquiring with it a little arithmetic also. 604

After dinner, a man believes less, denies more; verities have lost some charm. After dinner, arithmetic is the only science; ideas are disturbing, incendiary, follies of young men, repudiated by the solid portion of society; and a man comes to be valued by his athletic and animal qualities. 605

Life is eating us up. We shall be fables presently. Keep cool; it will be all one a hundred years hence. Life's well enough, but we shall be glad to get out of it, and they will all be glad to have us. 606

The studious class are their own victims; they are thin and pale, their feet are cold, their heads are hot, the night is without sleep, the day a fear of interruption,—pallor, squalor, hunger and egotism. 607

But I see plainly, he says, that I cannot see. I know that human strength is not in extremes, but in avoiding extremes. 608

Why be an angel before your time? 609

In short, since true fortitude of understanding consists "in not letting what we know be embarrassed by what we do not know," we ought to secure those advantages which we can command, and not risk them by clutching after the airy and unattainable.   610

The soul of man must be the type of our scheme, just as the body of man is the type after which a dwelling-house is built. Adaptiveness is the peculiarity of human nature.   611

The wise skeptic wishes to have a near view of the best game and the chief players; what is best in the planet; art and nature, places and events; but mainly men. Everything that is excellent in mankind,—a form of grace, an arm of iron, lips of persuasion, a brain of resources, every one skilful to play and win,—he will see and judge.   612

For the secrets of life are not shown except to sympathy and likeness. Men do not confide themselves to boys, or coxcombs, or pedants, but to their peers.   613

The sincerity and marrow of the man reaches to his sentences. I know not anywhere the book that seems less written. It is the language of conversation transferred to a book. Cut these word, and they would bleed; they are vascular and alive. (Montaigne's Essays.)   614

For blacksmiths and teamsters do not trip in their speech; it is a shower of bullets. It is Cambridge men who correct themselves and begin again at every half sentence, and, moreover, will pun, and refine too much, and swerve from the matter to the expression.   615

Montaigne talks with shrewdness, knows the world and books and himself, and uses the positive degree; never shrieks,

or protests, or prays; no weakness, no convulsion, no superlative; does not wish to jump out of his skin, or play any
antics, or annihilate space or time, but is stout and solid; tastes
every moment of the day; likes pain because it makes him feel
himself and realize things, as we pinch ourselves to know that
we are awake.   He keeps the plain; he rarely mounts or sinks;
likes to feel solid ground and the stones underneath.   His writing has no enthusiasms, no aspiration; contented, self-respecting
and keeping the middle of the road.   There is but one exception,—in his love for Socrates.   In speaking of him, for once
his cheek flushes and his style rises to passion.   616

We are natural believers.   Truth, or the connection between
cause and effect, alone interests us.   We are persuaded that a
thread runs through all things; all worlds are strung on it,
as beads; and men, and events, and life, come to us only because of that thread; they pass and repass only that we may
know the direction and continuity of that line.   A book or
statement which goes to show that there is no line, but random
and chaos, a calamity out of nothing, a prosperity and no account of it, a hero born from a fool, a fool from a hero,—
dispirits us.   Seen or unseen, we believe the tie exists.   Talent
makes counterfeit ties; genius finds the real ones.   We hearken
to the man of science, because we anticipate the sequence in
natural phenomena which he uncovers.   We love whatever affirms, connects, preserves; and dislike what scatters or pulls
down.   617

Skepticism is the attitude assumed by the student in relation
to the particulars which society adores, but which he sees to be
reverend only in their tendency and spirit.   The ground oc-
cupied by the skeptic is the vestibule of the temple.   618

Society does not like to have any breath of question blown
on the existing order.   But the interrogation of custom at all
points is an inevitable stage in the growth of every superior
mind, and is the evidence of its perception of the flowing power
which remain itself in all changes.   619

The wise skeptic is a bad citizen; no conservative, he sees the selfishness of property and the drowsiness of institutions. But neither is he fit to work with any democratic party that ever was constituted; for parties wish every one committed, and he penetrates the popular patriotism.   620

Knowledge is the knowing that we can not know. The dull pray; the geniuses are light mockers. How respectable is earnestness on every platform! but intellect kills it.   621

I think that the wiser a man is, the more stupendous he finds the natural and moral econo̧my, and lifts himself to a more absolute reliance.   622

Our life is March weather, savage and serene in one hour.
          623

In fact we may come to accept it as a fixed rule and theory of our state of education, that God is a substance, and his method is illusion.   624

The young spirit pants to enter society. But all the ways of culture and greatness lead to solitary imprisonment.   625

Belief consists in accepting the affirmations of the soul; unbelief, in denying them.   626

The skeptic denies out of more faith, and not less. He denies out of honesty. He had rather stand charged with the imbecility of skepticism, than with untruth. I believe, he says, in the moral design of the universe; it exists hospitably for the weal of souls; but your dogmas seem to me caricatures; why should I make believe them? Will any say, This is cold and infidel? The wise and magnanimous will not say so.
          627

The lesson of life is practically to generalize; to believe what the years and the centuries say, against the hours; to resist the usurpation of particulars; to penetrate to their catholic sense. Things seem to say one thing, and say the reverse. The appearance is immoral; the result is moral. Things seem to tend downward, to justify despondency, to promote rogues, to defeat the just; and by knaves as by martyrs the just cause is carried forward. Although knaves win in every political struggle, although society seems to be delivered over from the hands of one set of criminals into the hands of another set of criminals, as fast as the government is changed, and the march of civilization is a train of felonies,—yet general ends are somehow answered. 628

Let a man learn to look for the permanent in the mutable and fleeting; let him learn to bear the disappearance of things he was wont to reverence without losing his reverence; let him learn that he is here, not to work but to be worked upon; and that, though abyss open under abyss, and opinion displace opinion, all are at last contained in the Eternal Cause:—
"If my bark sink, 'tis to another sea." 629

SHAKESPEARE; OR, THE POET

(1564-1616 A. D.)

Great men are more distinguished by range and extent than by originality, *** no great men are original.   630

The greatest genius is the most indebted man.   631

It has come to be practically a sort of rule in literature, that a man having once shown himself capable of original writing, is entitled thenceforth to steal from the writings of others at discretion.   632

Thought is the property of him who can entertain it and of him who can adequately place it. A certain awkwardness marks the use of borrowed thoughts; but as soon as we have learned what to do with them they become our own.
Thus all originality is relative. Every thinker is retrospective.   633

It is easy to see that what is best written or done by genius in the world, was no man's work, but came by wide social labor, when a thousand wrought like one, sharing the same impulse.   634

Our English Bible is a wonderful specimen of the strength and music of the English language. But it was not made by one man, or at one time; but centuries and churches brought it to perfection. There never was a time when there was not some translation existing.   635

Grotius makes the like remark in respect to the Lord's Prayer, that the single clauses of which it is composed were already in use in the time of Christ, in the Rabbinical forms. He picked out the grains of gold.   636

The translation of Plutarch gets its excellence by being translation on translation. There never was a time when there was none. All the truly idiomatic and national phrases are kept, and all others successively picked out and thrown away.
637

A popular player;—nobody suspected he was the poet of the human race; and the secret was kept as faithfully from poets and intellectual men as from courtiers and frivolous people. Bacon, who took the inventory of the human understanding for his times, never mentioned his name. (Shakespeare).   638

Since the constellation of great men who appeared in Greece in the time of Pericles, there was never any such society;— (Shakespeare and contemporaries)—yet their genius failed them to find out the best head in the universe. Our poet's mask was impenetrable. You cannot see the mountain near.
639

It is the essence of poetry to spring, like the rainbow daughter of Wonder, from the invisible, to abolish the past and refuse all history.   640

Shakespeare is the only biographer of Shakespeare; and even he can tell nothing, except to the Shakespeare in us, that is, to our most apprehensive and sympathetic hour.   641

Hence, though our external history is so meagre, yet, with Shakespeare for biographer, instead of Aubrey and Rowe, we have really the information which is material; that which describes character and fortune, that which, if we were about to meet the man and deal with him, would most import us to know. We have his recorded convictions on those questions which knock for answer at every heart,—on life and death, on love, on wealth and poverty, on the prizes of life and the ways whereby we come at them; on the characters of men, and the influences, occult and open, which affect their fortunes; and on those mysterious and demoniacal powers which defy our science and which yet interweave their malice and their gift in our brightest hours.   642

So far from Shakespeare's being the least known, he is the one person, in all modern history, known to us.   643

He is like some saint whose history is to be rendered into all languages, into verse and prose, into songs and pictures, and cut up into proverbs; so that the occasion which gave the saint's meaning the form of a conversation, or of a prayer, or of a code of laws, is immaterial compared with the universality of its application. So it fares with the wise Shakespeare and his book of life. He wrote the airs for all our modern music; he wrote the text of modern life; the text of manners; he drew the man of England and Europe; the father of the man in America; he drew the man, and described the day, and what is done in it; he read the hearts of men and women, their probity, and their second thought and wiles; the wiles of innocence, and the transitions by which virtues and vices slide into their contraries; he could divide the mother's part from the father's part in the face of the child, or draw the fine demarcations of freedom and of fate; he knew the laws of repression which make the police of nature; and all the sweets and all the terrors of human lot lay in his mind as truly but as softly as the landscape lies on the eye.   644

Give a man of talents a story to tell, and his partiality will presently appear.   645

But Shakespeare has no peculiarity, no importunate topic; but all is duly given; no veins, no curiosities; no cow-painter, no bird-fancier, no mannerist is he; he has no discoverable egotism; the great he tells greatly; the small subordinately. He is wise without emphasis or assertion; he is strong, as nature is strong, who lifts the land into mountain slopes without effort and by the same rule as she floats a bubble in the air, and likes as well to do the one as the other. This makes that equality of power in farce, tragedy, narrative, and love-songs;

a merit so incessant that each reader is incredulous of the perception of other readers.   646

Things were mirrored in his poetry without loss or blur;
he could paint the fine with precision, the great with compass,
the tragic and the comic indifferently and without any dis-
tortion or favor.   He carried his powerful execution into
minute details, to a hair point; finishes an eyelash or a dimple
as firmly as he draws a mountain; and yet these, like nature's,
will bear the scrutiny of the solar microscope.   647

The finest poetry was first experience; but the thought has
suffered a transformation since it was an experience.   Cultivated men often attain a good degree of skill in writing verses;
but it is easy to read, through their poems, their personal
history.   648

He touches nothing that does not borrow health and
longevity from his festal style.   (of Shakespeare.)   649

He converted the elements which waited on his command,
into entertainments.   He was master of the revels to mankind.
                                                            650

Other admirable men have led lives in some sort of keeping
with their thought; but this man, in wide contrast.   651

But that this man of men, he who gave to the science of
mind a new and larger subject than had ever existed, and
planted the standard of humanity some furlongs forward into
Chaos,—that he should not be wise for himself;—it must
even go into the world's history that the best poet led an obscure and profane life, using his genius for the public amusement.   652

The world still wants its poet-priest, a reconciler, who shall
not trifle, with Shakespeare the player, nor shall grope in
graves, with Swedenborg the mourner; but who shall see,
speak, and act, with equal inspiration.   For knowledge will
brighten the sunshine; right is more beautiful than private affection; and love is compatible with universal wisdom.   653

SWEDENBORG; OR, THE MYSTIC
(1688-1772)

To the withered traditional church, yielding dry catechisms, he let in nature again, and the worshipper, escaping from the vestry of verbs and texts, is surprised to find himself a party to the whole of his religion. 654

Instead of a religion which visited him diplomatically three or four times,—when he was born, when he married, when he fell sick and when he died, and, for the rest, never interfered with him,—here was a teaching which accompanied him all day, accompanied him even into sleep and dreams; into his thinking, and showed him through what a long ancestry his thoughts descend; into society, and showed by what affinities he was girt to his equals and his counterparts; into natural objects, and showed their origin and meaning, what are friendly, and what are hurtful; and opened the future world by indicating the continuity of the same laws. 655

The moral insight of Swedenborg, the correction of popular errors, the announcement of ethical laws, take him out of comparison with any other modern writer and entitle him to a place, vacant for some ages, among the lawgivers of mankind. 656

Of course what is real and universal cannot be confined to the circle of those who sympathize strictly with his genius, but will pass forth into the common stock of wise and just thinking. The world has a sure chemistry, by which it extracts what is excellent in its children and lets fall the infirmities and limitations of the grandest mind. 657

All things in the universe arrange themselves to each person anew, according to his ruling love. Man is such as his affection and thought are. Man is man by virtue of willing, not by virtue of knowing and understanding. As he is, so he sees. 658

The Eden of God is bare and grand; like the outdoor land-scape remembered from the evening fireside, it seems cold and desolate whilst you cower over the coals, but once abroad again, we pity those who can forego the magnificence of nature for candle-light and cards.   659

We meet, and dwell an instant under the temple of one thought, and part, as though we parted not, to join another thought in other fellowships of joy. So far from there being anything divine in the low and proprietary sense of *Do you love me?* it is only when you leave and lose me by casting yourself on a sentiment which is higher than both of us, that I draw near and find myself at your side.   660

Success, or a fortunate genius, seems to depend on a happy adjustment of heart and brain.   661

Beauty is disgraced, love is unlovely, when truth, the half part of heaven, is denied, as much as when a bitterness in men of talent leads to satire and destroys the judgment.   662

The vice of Swedenborg's mind is its theologic determina-tion. Nothing with him has the liberality of universal wis-dom, but we are always in a church.   663

The genius of Swedenborg, largest of all modern souls in this department of thought, wasted itself in the endeavor to reanimate and conserve what had already arrived at its natural term, and, in the great secular Providence, was retiring from its prominence, before Western modes of thought and expres-sion. Swedenborg and Behmen both failed by attaching them-selvs to the Christian symbol, instead of to the moral senti-ment, which carries innumerable christianities, humanities, divinities, in its bosom.   664

He who loves goodness, harbors angels, reveres reverence and lives with God.   665

But the divine effort is never relaxed; the carrion in the sun will convert itself to grass and flowers; and man, though in brothels, or jails, or on the gibbets, is on his way to all that is good and true.   666

It is the best sign of a great nature that it opens a fore-ground, and, like the breath of morning landscapes, invites us onward.   667

Swedenborg has rendered a double service to mankind, which is now only beginning to be known. By the science of experi-ment and use, he made his first steps; he observed and pub-lished the laws of nature; and ascending by just degrees from events to their summits and causes, he was fired with piety at the harmonies he felt, and abandoned himself to his joy and worship. This was his first service. If the glory was too bright for his eyes to bear, if he staggered under the trance of delight, the more excellent is the spectacle he saw, the realities of being which beam and blaze through him, and which no infirmities of the prophet are suffered to obscure; and he renders a second passive service to men, not less than the first, perhaps, in the great circle of being,—and, in the retributions of spirit-ual nature, not less glorious or less beautiful to himself.   668

GOETHE; OR, THE WRITER

(1749-1832)

Every act of the man inscribes itself in the memories of his fellows and in his own manners and face. The air is full of sounds; the sky, of tokens; the round is all memoranda and signatures, and every object covered over with hints which speak to the intelligent.   669

Mankind have such a deep stake in inward illumination, that there is much to be said by the hermit or monk in defence of his life of thought and prayer.   670

For great action must draw on the spiritual nature. The measure of action is the sentiment from which it proceeds. The greatest action may easily be one of the most private circumstance.   671

Able men do not care in what kind a man is able, so only that he is able. A master likes a master, and does not stipulate whether it be orator, artist, craftsman, or king.   672

Society has really no graver interest than the well-being of the literary class.   673

The Helena, or the second part of Faust, is a philosophy of literature set in poetry; the work of one who found himself the master of histories, mythologies, philosophies, sciences and national literatures, in the encyclopædical manner in which modern erudition, with its international intercourse of the whole earth's population, researches into Indian, Etruscan and all Cyclopean arts; geology, chemistry, astronomy; and every one of these kingdoms assuming a certain aerial and poetic character, by reason of the multitude.   674

He was the soul of his century. . . . He has clothed our modern existence with poetry.   675

He has explained the distinction between the antique and the modern spirit and art. He has defined art, its scope and laws. He has said the best things about nature that ever were said.   676

Talent alone can not make a writer. There must be a man behind the book; a personality which by birth and quality is pledged to the doctrines there set forth.   677

It makes a great difference to the force of any sentence whether there be a man behind it or no. In the learned journal, in the influential newspaper, I discern no form; only some irresponsible shadow; oftener some moneyed corporation, or some dangler who hopes, in the mask and robes of his paragraph, to pass for somebody. But through every clause and part of speech of a right book I meet the eyes of the most determined of men; his force and terror inundate every word; the commas and dashes are alive; so that the writing is athletic and nimble,—can go far and live long.   678

The old Eternal Genius who built the world has confided himself more to this man than to any other.   679

I dare not say that Goethe ascended to the highest grounds from which genius has spoken. He has not worshipped the highest unity; he is incapable of a self-surrender to the moral sentiment. There are nobler strains in poetry than any he has sounded. There are writers poorer in talent, whose tone is purer, and more touches the heart. Goethe can never be dear to men. His is not even the devotion to pure truth; but to truth for the sake of culture.   680

This lawgiver of art is not an artist.   681

Goethe teaches courage, and the equivalence of all times;
that the disadvantages of any epoch exist only to the faint-
hearted.   Genius hovers with his sunshine and music close
by the darkest and deafest eras.   682

The secret of genius is to suffer no fiction to exist for us;
to realize all that we know; in the high refinement of modern
life, in arts, in sciences, in books, in men, to exact good faith,
reality and a purpose; and first, last, midst and without end,
to honor every truth by use.   683

NAPOLEON; OR, THE MAN OF THE WORLD

(1769-1821)

It is an advantage, within certain limits, to have renounced the dominion of the sentiments of piety, gratitude and generosity; since what was an impassable bar to us, and still is to others, becomes a convenient weapon for our purposes; just as the river which was a formidable barrier, winter transforms into the smoothest of roads.   684

Napoleon renounced, once for all, sentiments and affections, and would help himself with his hands and his head. With him is no miracle and no magic. He is a worker in brass, in iron, in wood, in earth, in roads, in buildings, in money and in troops, and a very consistent and wise master-workman. He is never weak and literary, but acts with the solidity and the precision of natural agents. He has not lost his native sense and sympathy with things. Men give way before such a man, as before natural events.   685

Therefore the land and sea seem to presuppose him. He came unto his own and they received him.   686

Nature must have far the greatest share in every success, and so in his. Such a man was wanted, and such a man was born; a man of stone and iron, capable of sitting on horseback sixteen or seventeen hours, of going many days together without rest or food except by snatches, and with the speed and spring of a tiger in action; a man not embarrassed by any scruples; compact, instant, selfish, prudent, and of a perception which did not suffer itself to be balked or misled by any pretences of others, or any superstition or any heat or haste of his own.   687

History is full, down to this day, of the imbecility of kings
and governors. They are a class of persons much to be pitied,
for they know not what they should do.   688

His victories were only so many doors, and he never for a
moment lost sight of his way onward, in the dazzle and uproar
of the present circumstance.   689

When a natural king becomes a titular king, every body is
pleased and satisfied.   690

Whatever appeals to the imagination, by transcending the
ordinary limits of human ability, wonderfully encourages and
liberates us.   691

The lesson he teaches is that which vigor always teaches;—
that there is always room for it.   692

I think all men know better than they do.   693

The democrat is a young conservative; the conservative is
an old democrat. The aristocrat is the democrat ripe and gone
to seed;—because both parties stand on the one ground of
the supreme value of property, which one endeavors to get, and
the other to keep.   694

Every experiment, by multitudes or by individuals, that has
a sensual and selfish aim, will fail.   695

As long as our civilization is essentially one of property,
of fences, of exclusiveness, it will be mocked by delusions. Our
riches will leave us sick; there will be bitterness in our laughter,
and our wine will burn our mouth. Only that good profits
which we can taste with all doors open, and which serves all
men.   696

CONDUCT OF LIFE
BEAUTY

From a great heart secret magnetisms flow incessantly to draw great events.   697

The motive of science was the extension of man, on all sides, into nature, till his hands should touch the stars, his eyes see through the earth, his ears understand the language of beast and bird, and the sense of the wind; and, through his sympathy, heaven and earth should talk with him.   698

Every spirit makes its house, and we can give a shrewd guess from the house to the inhabitant.   699

We say that every man is entitled to be valued by his best moment.   700

It (beauty) is the most enduring quality, and the most ascending quality.   701

In the true mythology Love is an immortal child, and Beauty leads him as a guide; nor can we express a deeper sense than when we say, Beauty is the pilot of the young soul.   702

In rhetoric, this art of omission is a chief secret of power, and, in general, it is proof of high culture to say the greatest matters in the simplest way.   703

A beautiful woman is a practical poet, taming her savage mate, planting tenderness, hope and eloquence in all whom she approaches.   704

It does not hurt weak eyes to look into beautiful eyes never so long.   705

Women stand related to beautiful nature around us, and the enamoured youth mixes their form with moon and stars, with woods and waters, and the pomp of summer. They heal us of awkwardness by their words and looks. We observe their intellectual influence on the most serious student. They refine and clear his mind; teach him to put a pleasing method into what is dry and difficult.   706

A beautiful person among the Greeks was thought to betray by this sign some secret favor of the immortal gods; and we can pardon pride, when a woman possesses such a figure that wherever she stands, or moves, or leaves a shadow on the wall, or sits for a portrait to the artist, she confers a favor on the world.   707

And yet—it is not beauty that inspires the deepest passion. Beauty without grace is the hook without the bait. Beauty, without expression tires.   708

Those who have ruled human destinies like planets for thousands of years, were not handsome men.   709

When the delicious beauty of lineaments loses its power, it is because a more delicious beauty has appeared; that an interior and durable form has been disclosed.   710

Things are pretty, graceful, rich, elegant, handsome, but, until they speak to the imagination, not yet beautiful.   711

If I could put my hand on the North Star, would it be as beautiful? The sea is lovely, but when we bathe in it the beauty forsakes all the near water. For the imagination and senses cannot be gratified at the same time.   712

All the facts in nature are nouns of the intellect, and make the grammar of the eternal language. Every word has a double, treble or centuple use and meaning.   713

There are no days in life so memorable as those which vibrated to some stroke of the imagination.   714

CONDUCT OF LIFE
BEHAVIOR

Nature tells every secret once. Yes, but in man she tells it all the time, by form, attitude, gesture, mien, face and parts of the face, and by the whole action of the machine. 715

Manners are very communicable; men catch them from each other. 716

Give a boy address and accomplishments and you give him the mastery of palaces and fortunes where he goes. 717

Wise men read very sharply all your private history in your look and gait and behavior. The whole economy of nature is bent on expression. The tell-tale body is all tongues. 718

The eyes of men converse as much as their tongues, with the advantage that the ocular dialect needs no dictionary, but is understood all the world over. 719

There are eyes, to be sure, that give no more admission into the man than blueberries. 720

It is very certain that each man carries in his eye the exact indication of his rank in the immense scale of men, and we are always learning to read it. A complete man should need no auxiliaries to his personal presence. 721

The maxim of courts is that manner is power. 722

Manners have been somewhat cynically defined to be a contrivance of wise men to keep fools at a distance. 723

The basis of good manners is self-reliance. Necessity is the law of all who are not self-possessed.   724

Manners require time, as nothing is more vulgar than haste.   725

There is some reason to believe that when a man does not write his poetry it escapes by other vents through him, instead of the one vent of writing; clings to his form and manners, whilst poets have often nothing poetical about them except their verses.   726

Society is the stage on which manners are shown; novels are the literature.   727

The man that stands by himself, the universe stands by him also.   728

How much we forgive to those who yield us the rare spectacle of heroic manners! We will pardon them the want of books, of arts, and even of the gentler virtues.   729

There is no beautifier of complexion, or form, or behavior, like the wish to scatter joy and not pain around us.   730

It is good to give a stranger a meal or a night's lodging. It is better to be hospitable to his good meaning and thought, and give courage to a companion.   731

CONDUCT OF LIFE

CONSIDERATIONS BY THE WAY

Nothing is impossible to the man who can will.   732

Mankind divides itself into two classes,—benefactors and malefactors. The second class is vast, the first a handful.   733

Shall we then judge a country by the majority, or by the minority? By the minority, surely.   734

Masses are rude, lame, unmade, pernicious in their demands and influence, and need not to be flattered but to be schooled.   735

The worst of charity is that the lives you are asked to preserve are not worth preserving.   736

If government knew how, I should like to see it check, not multiply the population.   737

In old Egypt it was established law that the vote of a prophet be reckoned equal to a hundred hands. I think it was much underestimated.   738

The more difficulty there is in creating good men, the more they are used when they come.   739

The mass are animal, in pupilage, and near chimpanzee.   740

Nature turns all malfeasance to good.   741

To say then, the majority are wicked, means no malice, no bad heart in the observer, but simply that the majority are unripe, and have not yet come to themselves, do not yet know their opinion.   742

The frost which kills the harvest of a year saves the harvests of a century, by destroying the weevil or the locust.   743

There is a tendency in things to right themselves, and the war or revolution or bankruptcy that shatters a rotten system, allows things to take a new and natural order.   744

Nature is upheld by antagonism.   745

The glory of character is in affronting the horrors of depravity to draw thence new nobilities of power.   746

A man of sense and energy, the late head of the Farm School in Boston Harbor, said to me, "I want none of your good boys, —give me the bad ones."   747

Mirabeau said, "There are none but men of strong passions capable of going to greatness; none but such capable of meriting the public gratitude."   748

But all great men come out of the middle classes. 'Tis better for the head; 'tis better for the heart.   749

A rich man was never in danger from cold, or hunger, or war, or ruffians,—and you can see he was not, from the moderation of his ideas.   750

We learn geology the morning after the earthquake.   751

Whenever you are sincerely pleased, you are nourished. The joy of the spirit indicates its strength. All healthy things are sweet-tempered. Genius works in sport, and goodness smiles to the last; and for the reason that whoever sees the law which distributes things, does not despond, but is animated to great desires and endeavors. He who desponds betrays that he has not seen it.   752

When there is sympathy, there needs but one wise man in a company and all are wise, so a blockhead makes a blockhead of his companion. Wonderful power to benumb possesses this brother.   753

Conversation is an art in which a man has all mankind for his competitors.   754

In excited conversation we have glimpses of the universe, hints of power native to the soul, far-darting lights and shadows of an Andes landscape, such as we can hardly attain in lone meditation.   755

Make yourself necessary to somebody. Do not make life hard to any.   756

Our prayers are prophets.   757

Sanity consists in not being subdued by your means.   758

The secret of culture is to learn that a few great points steadily reappear, alike in the poverty of the obscurest farm and in the miscellany of metropolitan life, and that these few are alone to be regarded;—the escape from all false ties; courage to be what we are, and love of what is simple and beautiful; independence and cheerful relation, these are the essentials,—these, and the wish to serve, to add somewhat to the well-being of men.   759

CONDUCT OF LIFE

CULTURE

A man is the prisoner of his power. A topical memory makes him an almanac; a talent for debate, a disputant; skill to get money makes him a miser, that is, a beggar. Culture reduces these inflammations by invoking the aid of other powers against the dominant talent, and by appealing to the rank of powers. It watches success. 760

It is said a man can write but one book; and if a man have a defect, it is apt to leave its impression on all his performances. 761

The pest of society is egotists. There are dull and bright, sacred and profane, coarse and fine egotists. 762

Beware of the man who says, "I am on the eve of a revelation." 763

Religious literature has eminent examples (of egotism) and if we run over our private list of poets, critics, philanthropists and philosophers, we shall find them infected with this dropsy and elephantiasis, which we ought to have tapped. 764

This goitre of egotism is so frequent among notable persons that we must infer some strong necessity in nature which it subserves. 765

He only is a well-made man who has a good determination. 766

Life is very narrow. Bring any club or company of intelligent men together again after ten years, and if the presence of some penetrating and calming genius could dispose them to frankness, what a confession of insanities would come up! 767

Culture is the suggestion, from certain best thoughts, that a man has a range of affinities through which he can modulate the violence of any master-tones that have a droning preponderance in his scale, and succor him against himself.   768

No performance is worth loss of geniality. 'Tis a cruel price we pay for certain fancy goods called fine arts and philosophy.
769

The hardiest skeptic who has seen a horse broken, a pointer trained, or who has visited a menagerie or the exhibition of the Industrious Fleas, will not deny the validity of education. "A boy," says Plato, "is the most vicious of all wild beasts;" and in the same spirit the old English poet Gascoigne says, "A boy is better unborn than untaught."   770

A great part of courage is the courage of having done the thing before.   771

Incapacity of melioration is the only mortal distemper.
* * They are past the help of surgeon or clergy.   772

Good criticism is very rare and always precious.   773

One of the benefits of a college education is to show the boy its little avail.   774

For the most part, only the light characters travel. Who are you that have no task to keep you at home?   775

No doubt, to a man of sense, travel offers advantages. As many languages as he has, as many friends, as many arts and trades, so many times is he a man.   776

You cannot have one well-bred man without a whole society of such. They keep each other up to any high point.   777

The mark of the man of the world is absence of pretension. He does not make a speech, he takes a low business-tone, avoids all brag, is nobody, dresses plainly, promises not at all, performs much, speaks in monosyllables, hugs his fact. He calls his employment by its lowest name, and so takes from evil tongues their sharpest weapon. 778

How the imagination is piqued by anecdotes of some great man passing incognito, as a king in gray clothes. 779

Whilst we want cities as the centres where the best things are found, cities degrade us by magnifying trifles. 780

Let us learn to live coarsely, dress plainly, and lie hard. The least habit of dominion over the palate has certain good effects not easily estimated. 781

There is a great deal of self-denial and manliness in poor and middle-class houses in town and country, that has not got into literature and never will, but that keeps the earth sweet; that saves on superfluities, and spends on essentials; that goes rusty and educates the boy; that sells the horse but builds the school; works early and late, takes two looms in the factory, three looms, six looms, but pays off the mortgage on the paternal farm, and then goes back cheerfully to work again. 782

Keep the town for occasions, but the habits should be formed to retirement. 783

Solitude, the safeguard of mediocrity, is, to genius, the stern friend, the cold, obscure shelter where moult the wings which will bear it farther than suns and stars. 784

He who should inspire and lead his race must be defended from travelling with the souls of other men, from living, breathing, reading and writing in the daily, time-worn yoke of their opinions. 785

The saint and poet seek privacy to ends the most public and universal, and it is the secret of culture to interest the man more in his public than in his private quality. 786

A man is a beggar who only lives to the useful, and however he may serve as a pin or rivet in the social machine, cannot be said to have arrived at self-possession.   787

A cheerful intelligent face is the end of culture, and success enough. For it indicates the purpose of nature and wisdom attained.   788

It is noticed that the consideration of the great periods and spaces of astronomy induces a dignity of mind and an indifference to death.   789

But there are higher secrets of culture, which are not for the apprentices but for proficients. These are lessons only for the brave. We must know our friends under ugly masks. The calamities are our friends.   790

The finished man of the world must eat of every apple once. He must hold his hatreds also at arm's length, and not remember spite. He has neither friends nor enemies, but values men only as channels of power.   791

Heaven sometimes hedges a rare character about with ungainliness and odium, as the burr that protects the fruit.   792

The longer we live the more we must endure the elementary existence of men and women; and every brave heart must treat society as a child, and never allow it to dictate.   793

The measure of a master is his success in bringing all men round to his opinion twenty years later.   794

Very few of our race can be said to be yet finished men. We still carry sticking to us some remains of the preceding inferior quadruped organization.   795

The time will come when the evil forms we have known can no more be organized. Man's culture can spare nothing, wants all the material. He is to convert all impediments into instruments, all enemies into power.   796

CONDUCT OF LIFE
FATE

To me, however, the question of the times resolved itself into a practical question of the conduct of life. How shall I live? We are incompetent to solve the times. Our geometry cannot span the huge orbits of the prevailing ideas, behold their return and reconcile their opposition. We can only obey our own polarity.   797

We are sure that, though we know not how, necessity does comport with liberty, the individual with the world, my polarity with the spirit of the times. The riddle of the age has for each a private solution.   798

But let us honestly state the facts. Our America has a bad name for superficialness. Great men, great nations, have not been boasters and buffoons, but perceivers of the terror of life, and have manned themselves to face it.   799

Savages cling to a local god of one tribe or town. The broad ethics of Jesus were quickly narrowed to village theologies, which preach an election or favoritism.   800

But Nature is no sentimentalist,—does not cosset or pamper us. We must see that the world is rough and surly, and will not mind drowning a man or a woman, but swallows your ship like a grain of dust.   801

The cold, inconsiderate of persons, tingles your blood, benumbs your feet, freezes a man like an apple.   802

The habit of the snake and spider, the snap of the tiger and other leapers and bloody jumpers, the crackle of the bones of his prey in the coil of the anaconda,—these are in the system, and

our habits are like theirs. You have just dined, and however
scrupulously the slaughter-house is concealed in the graceful
distance of miles, there is complicity, expensive races,—race living at the expense of race.   803

Without uncovering what does not concern us, or counting
how many species of parasites hang on a bombyx, or groping
after intestinal parasites or infusory biters, or the obscurities of
alternate generation,—the forms of the shark, the labrus, the
jaw of the sea-wolf paved with crushing teeth, the weapons of
the grampus, and other warriors hidden in the sea, are hints
of ferocity in the interiors of nature. Let us not deny it up and
down. Providence has a wild, rough, incalculable road to its
end, and it is of no use to try to whitewash its huge, mixed
instrumentalities, or to dress up that terrific benefactor in a
clean shirt and white neckcloth of a student in divinity.   804

Every spirit makes its house; but afterwards the house confines the spirit.
The gross lines are legible to the dull; the cabman is phre-
nologist so far, he looks in your face to see if his shilling is sure.
A dome of brow denotes one thing, a pot-belly another; a
squint, a pug-nose, mats of hair, the pigment of the epidermis,
betray character.   805

How shall a man escape from his ancestors?   806

In different hours a man represents each of several of his
ancestors, as if there were seven or eight of us rolled up in each
man's skin,—seven or eight ancestors at least, and they constitute the variety of notes for that new piece of music which his
life is.   807

In certain men digestion and sex absorb the vital force, and
the stronger these are, the individual is so much weaker. The
more of these drones perish, the better for the hive.   808

Hindoos say, "Fate is nothing but the deeds committed in a prior state of existence."   809

A good deal of our politics is physiological.   810

The book of Nature is the book of Fate. She turns the gigantic pages,—leaf after leaf,—never re-turning one. One leaf she lays down, a floor of granite; then a thousand ages, and a bed of slate; a thousand ages, and a measure of coal; a thousand ages, and a layer of marl and mud; vegetable forms appear; her first misshapen animals, zoöphyte, trilobium, fish; then, saurians,—rude forms, in which she has only blocked her future statue, concealing under these unwieldy monsters the fine type of her coming king. The face of the planet cools and dries, the races meliorate, and man is born. But when a race has lived its term, it comes no more again.   811

No picture of life can have any veracity that does not admit the odious facts. A man's power is hooped in by a necessity which, by many experiments, he touches on every side until he learns its arc.   812

The element running through entire nature, which we popularly call Fate, is known to us as limitation. Whatever limits us we call Fate.   813

As we refine, our checks become finer. If we rise to spiritual culture, the antagonism takes a spiritual form.   814

And last of all, high over thought, in the world of morals, Fate appears as vindicator, levelling the high, lifting the low, requiring justice in man, and always striking soon or late when justice is not done. What is useful will last, what is hurtful will sink.   815

But the lightning which explodes and fashions planets, maker of planets and suns, is in him (Man). On one side elemental order, sandstone and granite, rock-ledges, peat-bog, forest, sea and shore; and on the other part thought, the spirit which composes and decomposes nature,—here they are, side by side, god and devil, mind and matter, king and conspirator, belt and spasm, riding peacefully together in the eye and brain of every man.   816

So far as a man thinks, he is free.   817

The too much contemplation of these limits induces meanness. They who talk much of destiny, their birth-star, etc., are in a lower dangerous plane, and invite the evils they fear. 818

'Tis weak and vicious people who cast the blame on Fate. The right use of Fate is to bring up our conduct to the loftiness of nature.   819

If you believe in Fate to your harm, believe it at least for your good.   820

The day of days, the great day of the feast of life, is that in which the inward eye opens to the Unity in things, to the omnipresence of law;—sees that what is must be and ought to be, or is the best.   821

We hear eagerly every thought and word quoted from an intellectual man. But in his presence our own mind is roused to activity, and we forget very fast what he says.   822

A breath of will blows eternally through the universe of souls in the direction of Right and Necessity. It is the air which all intellects inhale and exhale, and it is the wind which blows the worlds into order and orbit.   823

Thought dissolves the material universe by carrying the mind up into a sphere where all is plastic.   824

If thought makes free, so does the moral sentiment. The mixtures of spiritual chemistry refuse to be analyzed.   825

Whoever has had experience of the moral sentiment cannot choose but believe in unlimited power. Each pulse from that heart is an oath from the Most High. I know not what the word *sublime* means, if it be not the intimations, in this infant, of a terrific force.   826

And one may say boldly that no man has a right perception of any truth who has not been reacted on by it so as to be ready to be its martyr.   827

The bulk of mankind believe in two gods. They are under one dominion here in the house, as friend and parent, in social circles, in letters, in art, in love, in religion; but in mechanics, in dealing with steam and climate, in trade, in politics, they think they come under another.   828

What good, honest, generous men at home, will be wolves and foxes on 'Change! What pious men in the parlor will vote for what reprobates at the polls! To a certain point, they believe themselves the care of a Providence. But in a steamboat, in an epidemic, in war, they believe a malignant energy rules.
829

Fate then is a name for facts not yet passed under the fire of thought; for causes which are unpenetrated.   830

But every jet of chaos which threatens to exterminate us is convertible by intellect into wholesome force. Fate is unpenetrated causes.   831

The annual slaughter from typhus far exceeds that of war; but right drainage destroys typhus. The plague in the sea-service from scurvy is healed by lemon juice and other diets portable or procurable; the depopulation by cholera and small-pox is ended by drainage and vaccination; and every other pest is not less in the chain of cause and effect, and may be fought off. And whilst art draws out the venom, it commonly extorts some benefit from the vanquished enemy. The mischievous torrent is taught to drudge for man; the wild beasts he makes useful for food, or dress, or labor; the chemic explosions are controlled like his watch. These are now the steeds on which he rides. Man moves in all modes, by legs of horses, by wings of wind, by steam, by gas of balloon, by electricity, and stands on tiptoe threatening to hunt the eagle in his own element.   832

Steam was till the other day the devil which we dreaded. Every pot made by any human potter or brazier had a hole in its cover, to let off the enemy, lest he should lift pot and roof and carry the house away.   833

A man must thank his defects, and stand in some terror of his talents. A transcendent talent draws so largely on his forces as to lame him; a defect pays him revenues on the other side.   834

Behind every individual closes organization; before him opens liberty,—the Better, the Best. The first and worse races are dead. The second and imperfect races are dying out, or remain for the maturing of higher. In the latest race, in man, every generosity, every new perception, the love and praise he extorts from his fellows, are certificates of advance out of fate into freedom.   835

Liberation of the will from the sheaths and clogs of organization which he has outgrown, is the end and aim of this world.
                                                                                      836

The pleasure of life is according to the man that lives it, and not according to the work or the place.   837

We know what madness belongs to love,—what power to paint a vile object in hues of heaven.   838

In youth we clothe ourselves with rainbows and go as brave as the zodiac.   In age we put out another sort of perspiration,— gout, fever, rheumatism, caprice, doubt, fretting and avarice. 839

A man's fortunes are the fruit of his character.   A man's friends are his magnetisms.   840

So each man, like each plant, has his parasites.   A strong, astringent, bilious nature has more truculent enemies than the slugs and moths that fret my leaves.   Such a one has curculios, borers, knife-worms; a swindler ate him first, then a client, then a quack, then smooth, plausible gentlemen, bitter and selfish as Moloch.   841

A good intention clothes itself with sudden power.   When a god wishes to ride, any chip or pebble will bud and shoot out winged feet and serve him for a horse.   842

Let us build altars to the Blessed Unity which holds nature and souls in perfect solution, and compels every atom to serve an universal end.   843

If in the least particular one could derange the order of nature, —who would accept the gift of life?   844

CONDUCT OF LIFE

ILLUSIONS

Life is a succession of lessons which must be lived to be understood.   845

Women, more than all, are the element and kingdom of illusion. Being fascinated, they fascinate.   846

We find a delight in the beauty and happiness of children that makes the heart too big for the body.   847

Life will show you masks that are worth all your carnivals.
                                                                                            848

And what avails it that science has come to treat space and time as simply forms of thought, and the material world as hypothetical, and withal our pretension of property and even of self-hood are fading with the rest, if, at last, even our thoughts are not finalities, but the incessant flowing and ascension reach these also, and each thought which yesterday was a finality, to-day is yielding to a larger generalization?   849

Whatever games are played with us, we must play no games with ourselves, but deal in our privacy with the last honesty and truth.   850

There is no chance and no anarchy in the universe. All is system and gradation. Every god is there sitting in his sphere. The young mortal enters the hall of the firmament; there is he alone with them alone, they pouring on him benedictions and gifts, and beckoning him up to their thrones. On the instant, and incessantly, fall snow-storms of illusions. He fancies himself in a vast crowd which sways this way and that and whose movement and doings he must obey; he fancies himself poor, orphaned, insignificant.   The mad crowd drives hither and thither, now furiously commanding this thing to be done, now that.   What is he that he should resist their will, and think or act for himself?   Every moment new changes and new showers of deceptions to baffle and distract him.   And when, by and by, for an instant, the air clears and the cloud lifts a little, there are the gods still sitting around him on their thrones,— they alone with him alone.   851

CONDUCT OF LIFE
POWER

Life is a search after power; and this is an element with which the world is so saturated,—there is no chink or crevice in which it is not lodged,—that no honest seeking goes unrewarded. 852

The key to the age may be this, or that, or the other, as the young orators describe; the key to all ages is—Imbecility; imbecility in the vast majority of men at all times, and even in heroes in all but certain eminent moments; victims of gravity, custom and fear. 853

The first wealth is health. 854

Shakespeare was theatre-manager and used the labor of many young men, as well as the playbooks. 855

A Western lawyer of eminence* said to me he wished it were a penal offense to bring an English law-book into a court in this country, so pernicious had he found in his experience our deference to English precedent. 856

(*Judge H. H. Emmons, Michigan, a relative of the Editor.)

As long as our people quote English standards they will miss the sovereignty of power. 857

The longer the drought lasts the more is the atmosphere surcharged with water. 858

It is an esoteric doctrine of society that a little wickedness is good to make muscle; as if conscience were not good for hands and legs; as if poor decayed formalists of law and order cannot run like wild goats, wolves, and conies; that as there is a use in medicine for poisons, so the world cannot move without rogues; that public spirit and the ready hand are as well found among the malignants. 859

Men of this surcharge of arterial blood cannot live on nuts, herb-tea, and elegies; cannot read novels and play whist; cannot satisfy all their wants at the Thursday Lecture or the Boston Athenæum. They pine for adventure, and must go to Pike's Peak; had rather die by the hatchet of a Pawnee than sit all day and every day at a counting-room desk. They are made for war, for the sea, for mining, hunting and clearing; for hairbreadth adventures, huge risks and the joy of eventful living. 860

In history the great moment is when the savage is just ceasing to be a savage, with all his hairy Pelasgic strength directed on his opening sense of beauty;—and you have Pericles and Phidias, not yet passed over into the Corinthian civility. Everything good in nature and the world is in that moment of transition, when the swarthy juices still flow plentifully from nature, but their astringency or acridity is got out by ethics and humanity. 861

The triumphs of peace have been in some proximity to war. 862

The affirmative class monopolize the homage of mankind. They originate and execute all the great feats.   863

Success goes thus invariably with a certain *plus* or positive power.   864

The one prudence in life is concentration; the one evil is dissipation.   865

Concentration is the secret of strength in politics, in war, in trade, in short in all management of human affairs.   866

There are twenty ways of going to a point, and one is the shortest; but set out at once on one.   867

The good judge is not he who does hair-splitting justice to every allegation, but who, aiming at substantial justice, rules something intelligible for the guidance of suitors.   The good lawyer is not the man who has an eye to every side and angle of contingency, and qualifies all his qualifications, but who throws himself on your part so heartily that he can get you out of a difficulty.   868

All the great speakers were bad speakers at first.   Stumping it through England for seven years made Cobden a consummate debater.   Stumping it through New England for twice seven trained Wendell Phillips.   869

CONDUCT OF LIFE

WEALTH

Every man is a consumer, and ought to be a producer. 870

Coal lay in ledges under the ground since the Flood, until a laborer with pick and windlass brings it to the surface. We may well call it black diamonds. Every basket is power and civilization. For coal is a portable climate. 871

He is the rich man who can avail himself of all men's faculties. He is the richest man who knows how to draw a benefit from the labors of the greatest number of men. 872

The subject of economy mixes itself with morals, inasmuch as it is a peremptory point of virtue that a man's independence be secured. Poverty demoralizes. A man in debt is so far a slave. 873

It is the privilege of any human work which is well done to invest the doer with a certain haughtiness. He can well afford not to conciliate, whose faithful work will answer for him. 874

To be rich is to have a ticket of admission to the masterworks and chief men of each race. It is to have the sea, by voyaging; to visit the mountains, Niagara, the Nile, the desert, Rome, Paris, Constantinople; to see galleries, libraries, arsenals, manufactories. 875

The world is his who has money to go over it. 876

They should own who can administer, not they who hoard and conceal; not they who, the greater proprietors they are, are only the greater beggars, but they whose work carves out work for more, opens a path for all. For he is the rich man in whom the people are rich, and he is the poor man in whom the people are poor; and how to give all access to the masterpieces of art and nature, is the problem of civilization.   877

The socialism of our day has done good service in setting men to thinking how certain civilizing benefits, now only enjoyed by the opulent, can be enjoyed by all.   878

In the Greek cities it was reckoned profane that any person should pretend a property in a work of art, which belonged to all who could behold it.   879

I think sometimes, could I only have music on my own terms; could I live in a great city and know where I could go whenever I wished the ablution and inundation of musical waves,—that were a bath and a medicine.   (Written 50 years before Radio.)   880

Man was born to be rich, or inevitably grows rich by the use of his faculties; by the union of thought with nature. Property is an intellectual production.   881

Cultivated labor drives out brute labor.   882

Every step of civil advancement makes every man's dollar worth more.   883

In Europe, crime is observed to increase or abate with the price of bread.   884

The basis of political economy is non-interference. The only safe rule is found in the self-adjusting meter of demand and supply.   885

Open the doors of opportunity to talent and virtue and they will do themselves justice. 886

Nature arms each man with some faculty which enables him to do easily some feat impossible to any other, and thus makes him necessary to society. 887

Nothing is beneath you, if it is in the direction of your life; nothing is great or desirable if it is off from that. 888

Let the realist not mind appearances. Let him delegate to others the costly courtesies and decorations of social life. The virtues are economists, but some of the vices are also. Thus, next to humility, I have noticed that pride is a pretty good husband. 889

Pride can go without domestics, without fine clothes, can live in a house with two rooms, can eat potato, purslane, beans, lyed corn, can work on the soil, can travel afoot, can talk with poor men, or sit silent well contented in fine saloons. But vanity costs money, labor, horses, men, women, health and peace, and is still nothing at last; a long way leading nowhere. Only one drawback; proud people are intolerably selfish, and the vain are gentle and giving. 890

Art is a jealous mistress, and if a man have a genius for painting, poetry, music, architecture or philosophy, he makes a bad husband and an ill provider, and should be wise in season and not fetter himself with duties which will embitter his days and spoil him for his proper work. 891

The secret of success lies never in the amount of money, but in the relation of income to outgo. 892

We say the cows laid out Boston. Well, there are worse surveyors. 893

Friendship buys friendship; justice, justice; military merit, military success. Good husbandry finds wife, children and household. The good merchant, large gains, ships, stocks and money. The good poet, fame and literary credit; but not either, the other.   894

The true thrift is always to spend on the higher plane; to invest and invest, with keener avarice, that he may spend in spiritual creation and not in augmenting animal existence. Nor is the man enriched, in repeating the old experiments of animal sensation; nor unless through new powers and ascending pleasures he knows himself by the actual experience of higher good to be already on the way to the highest.   895

CONDUCT OF LIFE

WORSHIP

The solar system has no anxiety about its reputation, and the credit of truth and honesty is as safe.   896

God builds his temple in the heart on the ruins of churches and religions.   897

The dogma of the mystic offices of Christ being dropped, and he standing on his genius as a moral teacher, it is impossible to maintain the old emphasis of his personality; and it recedes, as all persons must, before the sublimity of the moral laws.   898

Let a man attain the highest and broadest culture that any American has possessed, then let him die by sea-storm, railroad collision, or other accident, and all America will acquiesce that the best thing has happened to him; that, after the education has gone far, such is the expensiveness of America that the best use to put a fine person to is to drown him to save his board. 899

You say there is no religion now.   'Tis like saying in rainy weather, "There is no sun," when at that moment we are witnessing one of his superlative effects.   900

All the great ages have been ages of belief.   901

It is true that genius takes its rise out of the mountains of rectitude; that all beauty and power which men covet are somehow born out of that Alpine district; that any extraordinary degree of beauty in man or woman involves a moral charm. 902

There is an intimate interdependence of intellect and morals.
903

Skepticism is unbelief in cause and effect.   A man does not see that as he eats, so he thinks; as he deals, so he is, and so he appears; he does not see that his son is the son of his thoughts and of his actions; that fortunes are not exceptions but fruit; that relation and connection are not somewhere and sometimes, but everywhere and always; no miscellany, no exemption, no anomaly,—but method, and an even web; and what comes out, that was put in.   904

As we are, so we do; and as we do, so is it done to us; we are the builders of our fortunes.   905

Society is a masked ball, where every one hides his real character, and reveals it by hiding.   906

He is a strong man who can hold down his opinion.   A man cannot utter two or three sentences without disclosing to intelligent ears precisely where he stands in life and thought.   907

People seem not to see that their opinion of the world is also a confession of character.   908

The real and lasting victories are those of peace and not of war.   909

I look on that man as happy, who, when there is question of success, looks into his work for a reply, not into the market, not into opinion, not into patronage.   910

There was never a man born so wise or good but one or more companions came into the world with him, who delight in his faculty and report it.   I cannot see without awe that no man thinks alone and no man acts alone, but the divine assessors who came up with him into life,—now under one disguise, now under another, like a police in citizens' clothes,—walk with him, step for step, through all the kingdoms of time.   911

What I am and what I think is conveyed to you, in spite of my efforts to hold it back.   912

That only which we have within, can we see without.   If we meet no gods, it is because we harbor none.   If there is grandeur in you, you will find grandeur in porters and sweeps. He only is rightly immortal to whom all things are immortal.
913

Fear God, and where you go, men shall think they walk in hallowed cathedrals.   914

And so I look on those sentiments which make the glory of the human being, love, humility, faith, as being also the in- timacy of Divinity in the atoms; and that as soon as the man is right, assurances and previsions emanate from the interior of his body and his mind; as, when flowers reach their ripeness, incense exhales from them.   915

The moral equalizes all; enriches, empowers all.   It is the coin which buys all, and which all find in their pocket.   Under the whip of the driver, the slave shall feel his equality with saints and heroes.   916

Miracle comes to the miraculous, not to the arithmetician. 917

Of immortality, the soul when well employed is incurious. It is so well, that it is sure it will be well.   It asks no questions of the Supreme Power.   918

Immortality will come to such as are fit for it, and he who would be a great soul in future must be a great soul now.   It is a doctrine too great to rest on any legend, that is, on any man's experience but our own.   919

The religion which is to guide and fulfil the present and coming ages, whatever else it be, must be intellectual. The scientific mind must have a faith which is science. 920

Let us have nothing now which is not its own evidence. There is surely enough for the heart and imagination in the religion itself. Let us not be pestered with assertions and half-truths, with emotion and snuffle.

There will be a new church founded on moral science; at first cold and naked, a babe in the manger again, the algebra and mathematics of ethical law, the church of men to come, without shawms (horns) or psaltery*; but it will have heaven and earth for its beams and rafters; science for symbol and illustration; it will fast enough gather beauty, music, picture, poetry.** It shall send man home to his central solitude, shame these social, supplicating manners, and make him know that much of the time he must have himself to his friend.** The nameless Thought, the nameless Power, the super-personal Heart,—he shall repose alone on that.** Honor and fortune exist to him who always recognizes the neighborhood of the great—always feels himself in the presence of high causes. 921

SOCIETY AND SOLITUDE

'Tis worse, and tragic, that no man is fit for society who has fine traits. At a distance he is admired, but bring him hand to hand, he is a cripple.   922

Columbus discovered no isle or key so lonely as himself.   923

A scholar is a candle which the love and desire of all men will light.   924

The people are to be taken in very small doses.   If solitude is proud, so is society vulgar.   925

Society we must have; but let it be society, and not exchanging news or eating from the same dish.   926

All conversation is a magnetic experiment.   927

Society and solitude are deceptive names.   It is not the circumstance of seeing more or fewer people, but the readiness of sympathy, that imports.   928

SOCIETY AND SOLITUDE

CIVILIZATION

The most advanced nations are always those who navigate the most.   929

A man in a cave or in a camp, a nomad, will die with no more estate than the wolf or the horse leaves.   930

There can be no high civility without a deep morality.   931

The evolution of a highly destined society must be moral; it must run in the grooves of the celestial wheels.   932

The highest proof of civility is that the whole public action of the State is directed on securing the greatest good of the greatest number.   933

SOCIETY AND SOLITUDE

ART

Thought is the seed of action.   934

The universal soul is the alone creator of the useful and the beautiful; therefore to make anything useful or beautiful, the individual must be submitted to the universal mind.   935

The pleasure of eloquence is in greatest part owing often to the stimulus of the occasion which produces it,—to the magic of sympathy, which exalts the feeling of each by radiating on him the feeling of all.   936

The highest praise we can attribute to any writer, painter, sculptor, builder, is, that he actually possessed the thought or feeling with which he has inspired us.   937

The wonders of Shakespeare are things which he saw whilst he stood aside, and then returned to record them.   938

In eloquence, the great triumphs of the art are when the orator is lifted above himself; when consciously he makes himself the mere tongue of the occasion and the hour, and says what cannot but be said.   Hence the term *abandonment*, to describe the self-surrender of the orator.   939

Good poetry could not have been otherwise written than it is.   The first time you hear it, it sounds rather as if copied out of some invisible tablet in the Eternal mind than as if arbitrarily composed by the poet.   940

Herein is the explanation of the analogies, which exist in all the arts.   They are the re-appearance of one mind, working in

many materials to many temporary ends. Raphael paints wisdom, Handel sings it, Phidias carves it, Shakespeare writes it,
Wren builds it, Columbus sails it, Luther preaches it, Washington arms it, Watt mechanizes it. Painting was called "silent
poetry," and poetry "speaking painting." The laws of each
art are convertible into the laws of every other.   941

It never was in the power of any man or any community to
call the arts into being. They come to serve his actual wants,
never to please his fancy. These arts have their origin always in
some enthusiasm, as love, patriotism or religion. Who carved
marble? The believing man, who wished to symbolize their
gods to the waiting Greeks.   942

SOCIETY AND SOLITUDE
ELOQUENCE

Plato says that the punishment which the wise suffer who refuse to take part in the government, is, to live under the government of worse men.   943

There is no calamity which right words will not begin to redress.   944

There is also something excellent in every audience,—the capacity of virtue. They are ready to be beatified.   945

Perhaps it is the lowest of the qualities of an orator, but it is, on so many occasions, of chief importance,—a certain robust and radiant physical health; or,—shall I say?—great volumes of animal heat.   946

But in every constitution some large degree of animal vigor is necessary as material foundation for the higher qualities of the art.   947

The right eloquence needs no bell to call the people together, and no constable to keep them.   948

Eloquence is attractive as an example of the magic of personal ascendency,—a total and resultant power, rare, because it requires a rich coincidence of powers, intellect, will, sympathy, organs and, over all, good fortune in the cause.   949

A man who has tastes like mine, but in greater power, will rule me any day, and make me love my ruler.   950

Eloquence is the appropriate organ of the highest personal energy.   951

Eloquence must be grounded on the plainest narrative. After-wards, it may warm itself until it exhales symbols of every kind and color, speaks only through the most poetic forms; but first and last, it must still be at bottom a biblical statement of fact.   952

If you would lift me you must be on higher ground.   If you would liberate me you must be free.   953

He who will train himself to mastery in this science of per-suasion must lay the emphasis of education, not on popular arts, but on character and insight.   954

Eloquence, like every other art, rests on laws the most exact and determinate.   It is the best speech of the best soul.   955

SOCIETY AND SOLITUDE

DOMESTIC LIFE

What art can paint or gild any object in after-life with the glow which Nature gives to the first baubles of childhood.   956

The great facts are the near ones.   The account of the body is to be sought in the mind.   The history of your fortunes is written first in your life.   957

Honor to the house where they are simple to the verge of hardship, so that there the intellect is awake and reads the laws of the universe, the soul worships truth and love, honor and courtesy flow into all deeds.   958

It is the iron band of poverty, of necessity, of austerity, which, excluding them (poor boys) from the sensual enjoyments which make other boys too early old, has directed their activity in safe and right channels, and made them, despite themselves, reverers of the grand, the beautiful and the good.   959

How seldom do we behold tranquillity!   We have never yet seen a man.   960

Happy will that house be in which the relations are formed from character; after the highest, and not after the lowest order; the house in which character marries, and not confusion and a miscellany of unavowable motives.   961

The ornament of a house is the friends who frequent it.   962

Whatever brings the dweller into a finer life, what educates his eye, or ear, or hand, whatever purifies and enlarges him, may well find place there (in the household).   And yet let him not think that a property in beautiful objects is necessary to his apprehension of them, and seek to turn his house into a museum.   963

The fountain of beauty is the heart, and every generous thought illustrates the walls of your chamber.   964

Whoso shall teach me how to eat my meat and take my repose and deal with men, without any shame following, will restore the life of man to splendor, and make his own name dear to all history.   965

SOCIETY AND SOLITUDE

FARMING

The glory of the farmer is that, in the division of labors, it is his part to create. All trade rests at last on his primitive activity.   966

The first farmer was the first man.   967

The farmer is a hoarded capital of health, as the farm is the capital of wealth; and it is from him that the health and power, moral and intellectual, of the cities came. The city is always recruited from the country. The men in cities who are the centres of energy, the driving-wheels of trade, politics or practical arts, and the women of beauty and genius, are the children or grandchildren of farmers, and are spending the energies which their fathers' hardy, silent life accumulated in frosty furrows, in poverty, necessity and darkness.   968

Nations burn with internal fire of thought and affection, which wastes while it works. We shall find finer combustion and finer fuel. Intellect is a fire; rash and pitiless it melts this wonderful bone-house which is called man. Genius even, as it is the greatest good, is the greatest harm.   969

The farmer stands well on the world. Plain in manners as in dress, he would not shine in palaces; he is absolutely unknown and inadmissible therein; living or dying, he never shall be heard of in them; yet the drawing-room heroes put down beside him would shrivel in his presence.   970

SOCIETY AND SOLITUDE
WORKS AND DAYS

These arts (new inventions) open great gates of a future, promising to make the world plastic and to lift human life out of its beggary to a god-like ease and power. 971

Every new step in improving the engine restricts one more act of the engineer,—unteaches him. 972

'Tis too plain that with the material power the moral progress has not kept pace. It appears that we have not made a judicious investment. Works and days were offered us, and we took works. 973

He only is rich who owns the day. 974

The days are ever divine as to the first Aryans. They are of the least pretension and of the greatest capacity of anything that exists. They come and go like muffled and veiled figures, sent from a distant friendly party; but they say nothing, and if we do not use the gifts they bring, they carry them as silently away. 975

There are days when the great are near us, when there is no frown on their brow, no condescension even; when they take us by the hand, and we share their thought. 976

Hume's doctrine was that the circumstances vary, the amount of happiness does not; that the beggar cracking fleas in the sunshine under a hedge, and the duke rolling by in his chariot; the girl equipped for her first ball, and the orator returning triumphant from the debate, had different means, but the same quantity of pleasant excitement. 977

This element of illusion lends all its force to hide the values of present time.   978

One of the illusions is that the present hour is not the critical, decisive hour. Write it on your heart that every day is the best day in the year. No man has learned anything rightly until he knows that every day is Doomsday.   979

'Tis the old secret of the gods that they come in low disguises. 'Tis the vulgar great who come dizened with golds and jewels. Real kings hide away their crowns in their wardrobes, and affect a plain and poor exterior.   980

We owe to genius always the same debt, of lifting the curtain from the common, and showing us that divinities are sitting disguised in the seeming gang of gypsies and peddlers.   981

In daily life what distinguishes the master is the using those materials he has, instead of looking about for what are more renowned, or what others have used well.   982

The highest heaven of wisdom is alike near from every point, and thou must find it, if at all, by methods native to thyself alone.   983

The reverence for the deeds of our ancestors is a treacherous sentiment.   984

A song is no song unless the circumstance is free and fine. If the singer sing from a sense of duty or from seeing no way to escape, I had rather have none. Those only can sleep who do not care to sleep; and those only write or speak best who do not too much respect the writing or the speaking.   985

SOCIETY AND SOLITUDE
BOOKS

Consider what you have in the smallest chosen library. A company of the wisest and wittiest men that could be picked out of all civil countries in a thousand years have set in best order the results of their learning and wisdom. The men themselves were hid and inaccessible, solitary, impatient of interruption, fenced by etiquette; but the thought which they did not uncover to their bosom friend is here written out in transparent words to us, the strangers of another age. 986

We owe to books those general benefits which come from high intellectual action. 987

All books that get fairly into the vital air of the world were written by the successful class, by the affirming and advancing class, who utter what tens of thousands feel though they cannot say. 988

The three practical rules, then, which I have to offer, are,— 1. Never read any book that is not a year old. 2. Never read any but famed books. 3. Never read any but what you like. 989

I rarely read any Latin, Greek, German, Italian, sometimes not a French book, in the original, which I can procure in a good version. I like to be beholden to the great metropolitan English speech, the sea which receives tributaries from every region under heaven. I should as soon think of swimming across Charles River when I wish to go to Boston, as of reading all my books in originals when I have them rendered for me in my mother tongue. 990

This passion for romance, and this disappointment, show
how much we need real elevations and pure poetry; that which
shall show us, in morning and night, in stars and mountains
and in all the plight and circumstance of men, the analogons of
our own thoughts, and a like impression made by a just book
and by the face of Nature.   991

SOCIETY AND SOLITUDE
CLUBS

We seek society with very different aims, and the staple of conversation is widely unlike in its circles. Sometimes it is facts, —running from those of daily necessity, to the last results of science,— and has all degrees of importance; sometimes it is love, and makes the balm of our early and of our latest days; sometimes it is thought, as from a person who is a mind only; sometimes a singing, as if the heart poured out all like a bird; sometimes experience. 992

Neither do we by any means always go to people for conversation. How often to say nothing,—and yet must go; as a child will long for his companions, but among them plays by himself. 993

Thought is the child of the intellect. 994

Nothing seems so cheap as the benefit of conversation; nothing is more rare. 995

Conversation in society is found to be on a platform so low as to exclude science, the saint and the poet. Amidst all the gay banter, sentiment cannot profane itself and venture out. 996

Some men love only to talk where they are masters. 997

Conversation is the vent of character as well as of thought. 998

To answer a question so as to admit of no reply, is the test of a man.   999

The best conversation is rare.   Society seems to have agreed to treat fictions as realities, and realities as fictions; and the simple lover of truth, especially if on very high grounds, as a religious or intellectual seeker, finds himself a stranger and alien.
1000

The man of thought, the man of letters, the man of science, the administrator skilful in affairs, the man of manners and culture, whom you so much wish to find,—each of these is wishing to be found.   Each wishes to open his thought, his knowledge, his social skill to the daylight in your company and affection, and to exchange his gifts for yours; and the first hint of a select and intelligent company is welcome.   1001

A right rule for a club would be,—Admit no man whose presence excludes any one topic.   1002

Discourse, when it rises highest and searches deepest, when it lifts us into that mood out of which thoughts come that remain as stars in our firmanent, is between two.   1003

SOCIETY AND SOLITUDE
COURAGE

There are three qualities which conspicuously attract the wonder and reverence of mankind:—1. Disinterestedness, as shown in indifference to the ordinary bribes and influences of conduct,—a purpose so sincere and generous that it cannot be tempted aside by any prospects of wealth or other private advantage. ** 2. Practical Power. Men admire the man who can organize their wishes and thoughts in stone and wood and steel and brass. ** 3. The third excellence is Courage, the perfect will, which no terrors can shake, which is attracted by frowns or threats or hostile armies, nay, needs these to awake and fan its reserved energies into a pure flame, and is never quite itself until the hazard is extreme; then it is serene and fertile, and all its powers play well.   1004

'Tis said courage is common, but the immense esteem in which it is held proves it to be rare.   1005

Men are so charmed with valor that they have pleased themselves with being called lions, leopards, eagles and dragons. 1006

Cowardice shuts the eyes till the sky is not larger than a calf-skin; shuts the eyes so that we cannot see the horse that is running away with us; worse, shuts the eyes of the mind and chills the heart. Fear is cruel and mean. The political reigns of terror have been reigns of madness and malignity,—a total perversion of opinion; society is upside down, and its best men are thought too bad to live.   1007

Nature has made up her mind that what cannot defend itself shall not be defended.   1008

Knowledge is the antidote to fear. ** Knowledge, yes; for the danger of dangers is illusion.   1009

Pain is superficial, and therefore fear is.   The torments of martyrdoms are probably most keenly felt by the by-standers.
1010

The dog that scorns to fight, will fight for his master.   The llama that will carry a load if you caress him, will refuse food and die if he is scourged.   The fury of onset is one, and of calm endurance another.   1011

There is a courage in the treatment of every art by a master in architecture, in sculpture, in painting or in poetry, each cheering the mind of the spectator or receiver as by true strokes of genius, which yet nowise implies the presence of physical valor in the artist.   This is the courage of genius, in every kind. 1012

The old principles which books exist to express are more beautiful than any book; and out of love of the reality he is an expert judge how far the book has approached it and where it has come short.   1013

Everything feels the new breath (of courage) except the old doting nigh-dead politicians, whose heart the trumpet of resurrection could not awake.   1014

There is a persuasion in the soul of man that he is here for cause, that he was put down in this place by the Creator to do the work for which he inspires him, and thus he is an overmatch for all antagonists that could combine against him.   1015

There are ever appearing in the world men who, almost as
soon as they are born, take a bee-line to the rack of the inquisi-
tor, the axe of the tyrant, like Giordano Bruno, Vanini, Huss,
Paul, Jesus and Socrates.   Look at Fox's Lives of the Martyrs,
Sewel's History of the Quakers, Southey's Book of the Church,
at the folios of the Brothers Bollandi, who collected the lives
of twenty-five thousand martyrs, confessors, ascetics and self-
tormentors.   There is much of fable, but a broad basis of fact.
The tender skin does not shrink from bayonets, the timid
woman is not scared by fagots; the rack is not frightful, nor the
rope ignominious.   1016

There are degrees of courage, and each step upward makes us
acquainted with a higher virtue.   Let us say then frankly that
the education of the will is the object of our existence.   1017

In the most private life, difficult duty is never far off.   Therefore we must think with courage.   1018

Scholars and thinkers are prone to an effeminate habit, and
shrink if a coarser shout comes up from the street, or a brutal
act is recorded in the journals.   The Medical College piles up
in its museum its grim monsters of morbid anatomy, and there
are melancholy skeptics with a taste for carrion who batten on
the hideous facts in history,—persecutions, inquisitions, St.
Bartholomew massacres, devilish lives, Nero, Caesar Borgia,
Marat, Lopez; men in whom every ray of humanity was ex-
tinguished, parricides, matricides and whatever moral monsters.
These are not cheerful facts, but they do not disturb a healthy
mind; they require of us a patience as robust as the energy that
attacks us, and an unresting exploration of final causes.   1019

SOCIETY AND SOLITUDE
SUCCESS

We respect ourselves more if we have succeeded. 1020

The public values the invention more than the inventor does. The inventor knows there is much more and better where this came from. 1021

I hate this shallow Americanism which hopes to get rich by credit, to get knowledge by raps on midnight tables, to learn the economy of the mind by phrenology, or skill without study, or mastery without apprenticeship, or the sale of goods through pretending that they sell, or power through making believe you are powerful, or through a packed jury or caucus, bribery and "repeating" votes, or wealth by fraud. 1022

Each man has an aptitude born with him. Do your work. 1023

The gravest and learnedest courts in this country shudder to face a new question, and will wait months and years for a case to occur that can be tortured into a precedent, and thus throw on a bolder party the *onus* of an initiative. 1024

Self-trust is the first secret of success. 1025

It is sanity to know that, over my talent or knack, and a million times better than any talent, is the central intelligence which subordinates and uses all talents; and it is only as a door into this, that any talent or the knowledge it gives is of value. 1026

[169]

There is something of poverty in our criticism.   1027

The light by which we see in this world comes out from the soul of the observer.   1028

We live among gods of our own creation.   1029

The fundamental fact in our metaphysic constitution is the correspondence of man to the world, so that every change in that writes a record in the mind.   The mind yields sympathetically to the tendencies or law which stream through things and make the order of Nature; and in the perfection of this correspondence or expressiveness, the health and force of man consist.   If we follow this hint into our intellectual education, we shall find that it is not propositions, not new dogmas and a logical exposition of the world that are our first need; but to watch and tenderly cherish the intellectual and moral sensibilities, those fountains of right thought, and woo them to stay and make their home with us.   Whilst they abide with us we shall not think amiss.   Our perception far outruns our talent.   We bring a welcome to the highest lessons of religion and of poetry out of all proportion beyond our skill to teach.

Every man has a history worth knowing, if he could tell it, or if we could draw it from him.   Character and wit have their own magnetism.   1031

Health is the condition of wisdom, and the sign is cheerfulness,—an open and noble temper.   There was never poet who had not the heart in the right place.   1032

The plenty of the poorest place is too great; the harvest cannot be gathered. Every sound ends in music. The edge of every surface is tinged with prismatic rays.   1033

We know the Spirit by its victorious tone.   1034

I fear the popular notion of success stands in direct opposition in all points to the real and wholesome success. One adores public opinion, the other, private opinion; one, fame, the other, desert; one, feats, the other, humility; one, lucre, the other, love; one, monopoly, and the other, hospitality of mind.   1035

Don't hang a dismal picture on the wall, and do not daub with sables and glooms in your conversation. Don't be a cynic and a disconsolate preacher. Don't bewail and bemoan. Omit the negative propositions. Nerve us with incessant affirmatives. Don't waste yourself in rejection, nor bark against the bad, but chant the beauty of the good. When that is spoken which has a right to be spoken, the chatter and the criticism will stop. Set down nothing that will not help somebody;—
    "For every gift of noble origin
    Is breathed upon by Hope's perpetual breath."
                1036

The affirmative of affirmatives is love. As much love, so much perception. As caloric to matter, so is love to mind; so it enlarges, and so it empowers it. Good will makes insight, as one finds his way to the sea by embarking on a river.   1037

SOCIETY AND SOLITUDE
OLD AGE

Time is indeed the theatre and seat of illusion; nothing is so ductile and elastic. The mind stretches an hour to a century and dwarfs an age to an hour.   1038

We postpone our literary work until we have more ripeness and skill to write, and we one day discover that our literary talent was a youthful effervescence which we have now lost.   1039

A third felicity of age is that it has found expression. The youth suffers not only from ungratified desires, but from powers untried, and from a picture in his mind of a career which has as yet no outward reality. He is tormented with the want of correspondence between things and thoughts.   1040

In old persons, we often observe a fair, plump, perennial, waxen complexion, which indicates that all the ferment of earlier days has subsided into serenity of thought and behavior.   1041

When life has been well spent, age is a loss of what it can well spare,—muscular strength, organic instincts, gross bulk, and works that belong to these. But the central wisdom, which was old in infancy, is young in fourscore years, and dropping off obstructions, leaves in happy subjects the mind purified and wise.   1042

I have heard that whoever loves is in no condition old. I
have heard that whenever the name of man is spoken, the doctrine of immortality is announced; it cleaves to his constitution.
The mode of it baffles our wit, and no whisper comes to us
from the other side. But the inference from the working of intellect, hiving knowledge, hiving skill,—at the end of life just
ready to be born,—affirms the inspirations of affection and of
the moral sentiment.   1043

POETRY AND IMAGINATION

The ends of all are moral, and therefore the beginnings are such. Thin or solid, everything is in flight. I believe this conviction makes the charm of chemistry. 1044

The hardest chemist, the severest analyzer, scornful of all but dryest fact, is forced to keep the poetic curve of Nature, and his result is like a myth of Theocritus. All multiplicity rushes to be resolved into unity. 1045

The world is an immense picture-book of every passage in human life. Every object he beholds is the mask of a man. 1046

Every correspondence we observe in mind and matter suggests a substance older and deeper than either of these old nobilities. 1047

Science does not know its debt to imagination. Goethe did not believe that a great naturalist could exist without this faculty. 1048

God himself does not speak prose, but communicates with us by hints, omens, inference and dark resemblances in objects lying all around us. 1049

Nothing so marks a man as imaginative expression. A figurative statement arrests attention, and is remembered and repeated. 1050

A happy symbol is a sort of evidence that your thought is just.   1051

Poetry is the perpetual endeavor to express the spirit of the thing, to pass the brute body and search the life and reason which causes it to exist;—to see that the object is always flowing away, whilst the spirit or necessity which causes it subsists.
1052

The very design of imagination is to domesticate us in another, in a celestial nature.   1053

I think the use or value of poetry to be the suggestion it affords of the flux or fugaciousness of the poet.   1054

The poet has a logic, though it be subtle.   He observes higher laws than he transgresses.   1055

A man's action is only a picture-book of his creed.   He does after what he believes.   Your condition, your employment, is the fable of *you.*   1056

It is a rule in eloquence, that the moment the orator loses command of his audience, the audience commands him.   1057

In dreams we are true poets; we create the persons of the drama; we give them appropriate figures, faces, costume; they are perfect in their organs, attitude, manners; moreover they speak after their own characters, not ours;—they speak to us, and we listen with surprise to what they say.   1058

The verse must be alive, and inseparable from its contents, as
the soul of man inspires and directs the body, and we measure
the inspiration by the music. In reading prose, I am sensitive
as soon as a sentence drags; but in poetry, as soon as one word
drags.   1059

Is not poetry the little chamber in the brain where is gen-
erated the explosive force which, by gentle shocks, sets in action
the intellectual world?   1060

The supreme value of poetry is to educate us to a height beyond itself; or which it rarely reaches;—the subduing mankind
to order and virtue.   1061

The problem of the poet is to unite freedom with precision;
to give the pleasure of color, and be not less the most powerful
of sculptors.   1062

Poetry is inestimable as a lonely faith, a lonely protest in the
uproar of atheism.   1063

Sooner or later that which is now life shall be poetry, and
every fair and manly trait shall add a richer strain to the song.
                                                            1064

SOCIAL AIMS

Manners are the revealers of secrets, the betrayers of any disproportion or want of symmetry in mind and character. 1065

It is the law of our constitution that every change in our experience instantly indicates itself on our countenance and carriage, as the lapse of time tells itself on the face of a clock. We may be too obtuse to read it, but the record is there. Some men may be obtuse to read it, but some men are not obtuse and do read it. 1066

Life is not so short but that there is always time enough for courtesy. 1067

Thus a king or a general does not need a fine coat, and a commanding person may save himself all solicitude on that point. 1068

If a man have manners and talent he may dress roughly and carelessly. It is only when mind and character slumber that the dress can be seen. 1069

I have heard with admiring submission the experience of the lady who declared that "the sense of being perfectly well dressed gives a feeling of inward tranquillity which religion is powerless to bestow." 1070

In this art of conversation, Woman, if not the queen and victor, is the lawgiver.   If every one recalled his experiences, he might find the best in the speech of superior women.   1071

No one can be a master in conversation who has not learned much from women; their presence and inspiration are essential to its success.   1072

Good manners are made up of petty sacrifices.   Temperance, courage, love, are made up of the same jewels.   1073

Those people, and no others, interest us, who believe in their thought, who are absorbed, if you please to say so, in their own dream.   1074

ELOQUENCE

We reckon the bar, the senate, journalism and the pulpit, peaceful professions; but you cannot escape the demand for courage in these, and certainly there is no true orator who is not a hero. 1075

The voice, indeed, is a delicate index of the state of mind. 1076

If I should make the shortest list of the qualifications of the orator, I should begin with *manliness;* and perhaps it means here presence of mind. 1077

Eloquence is the power to translate a truth into language perfectly intelligible to the person to whom you speak. 1078

When a great sentiment, as religion or liberty, makes itself deeply felt in any age or country, then great orators appear.
If there ever was a country where eloquence was a power, it is the United States. Here is room for every degree of it, on every one of its ascending stages,—that of useful speech, in our commercial, manufacturing, railroad and educational conventions; that of political advice and persuasion on the grandest theatre, reaching, as all good men trust, into a vast future, and so compelling the best thought and noblest administrative ability that the citizen can offer. 1079

RESOURCES

A low, hopeless spirit puts out the eyes; skepticism is slow suicide. A philosophy which sees only the worst; believes neither in virtue nor in genius; which says 'tis all of no use, life is eating us up, 'tis only question who shall be last devoured,—dispirits us; the sky shuts down before us.   1080

A Schopenhauer, with logic and learning and wit, teaching pessimism,—teaching that this is the worst of all possible worlds, and inferring that sleep is better than waking, and death than sleep,—all the talent in the world cannot save him from being odious. But if instead of these negatives you give me affirmatives; if you tell me that there is always life for the living; that what man has done man can do; that this world belongs to the energetic; that there is always a way to everything desirable; that every man is provided, in the new bias of his faculty, with a key to Nature, and that man only rightly knows himself as far as he has experimented on things, —I am invigorated, put into genial and working temper; the horizon opens, and we are full of good will and gratitude to the Cause of Causes.   1081

The world belongs to the energetic man. His will gives him new eyes.   1082

THE COMIC

A taste for fun is all but universal in our species, which is the only joker in Nature.   1083

Reason does not joke, and men of reason do not; a prophet, in whom the moral sentiment predominates, or a philosopher, in whom the love of truth predominates, these do not joke, but they bring the standard, the ideal whole, exposing all actual defect; and hence the best of all jokes is the sympathetic contemplation of things by the understanding from the philosopher's point of view.   1084 .

There is no joke so true and deep in actual life as when some pure idealist goes up and down among the institutions of society, attended by a man who knows the world, and who, sympathizing with the philosopher's scrutiny, sympathizes also with the confusion and indignation of the detected, skulking institutions. His perception of disparity, his eye wandering perpetually from the rule to the crooked, lying, thieving fact, makes the eyes run over with laughter.

This is the radical joke of life and then of literature.   1085

The presence of the ideal of right and of truth in all action makes the yawning delinquencies of practice remorseful to the conscience, tragic to the interest, but droll to the intellect.   1086

A perception of the Comic seems to be a balance-wheel in our metaphysical structure. It appears to be an essential element in a fine character. Wherever the intellect is constructive, it will be found. We feel the absence of it as a defect in the noblest and most oracular soul.   1087

The perception of the Comic is a tie of sympathy with other men, a pledge of sanity, and a protection from those perverse tendencies and gloomy insanities in which fine intellects sometimes lose themselves. A rogue alive to the ludicrous is still convertible. If that sense is lost, his fellow men can do little for him.   1088

Wit makes its own welcome, and levels all distinctions. No dignity, no learning, no force of character, can make any stand against good wit.   1089

The oldest gibe of literature is the ridicule of false religion. This is the joke of jokes.   1090

QUOTATION AND ORIGINALITY

Our high respect for a well-read man is praise enough of literature.   1091

In a large sense, one would say there is no pure originality. All minds quote. Old and new make the warp and woof of every moment. There is no thread that is not a twist of these two strands. By necessity, by proclivity and by delight, we all quote. We quote not only books and proverbs, but arts, sciences, religion, customs and laws; nay, we quote temples and houses, tables and chairs by imitation.   1092

If we confine ourselves to literature, 'tis easy to see that the debt is immense to past thought. None escapes it. The originals are not original. There is imitation, model and suggestion, to the very archangels, if we knew their history.   1093

A great man quotes bravely, and will not draw on his invention when his memory serves him with a word as good.
1094

Next to the originator of a good sentence is the first quoter of it.   1095

Genius borrows nobly.   1096

Observe also that a writer appears to more advantage in the pages of another book than in his own. In his own he waits as a candidate for your approbation; in another's he is a lawgiver.   1097

Goethe frankly said, "What would remain to me if this art of appropriation were derogatory to genius? Every one of my writings has been furnished to me by a thousand different persons, a thousand things."   1098

Only an inventor knows how to borrow, and every man is or should be an inventor. * * This vast memory is only raw material. The divine gift is ever the instant life, which receives and uses and creates, and can well bury the old in the omnipotency with which Nature decomposes all her harvest for recomposition.   1099

PROGRESS OF CULTURE

A controlling influence of the times has been the wide and successful study of Natural Science. 1100

The narrow sectarian cannot read astronomy with impunity. The creeds of his church shrivel like dried leaves at the door of the observatory, and a new and healthful air regenerates the human mind, and imparts a sympathetic enlargement to its inventions and method. 1101

Nothing is old but the mind. 1102

It is a curious fact that a certain enormity of culture makes a man invisible to his contemporaries. It is always hard to go beyond your public. 1103

But, from time to time in history, men are born a whole age too soon. 1104

Culture implies all which gives the mind possession of its own powers; as languages to the critic, telescope to the astronomer. 1105

Literary history and all history is a record of the power of minorities, and of minorities of one. Every book is written with a constant secret reference to the few intelligent persons whom the writer believes to exist in the million. The artist has always the masters in his eye, though he affect to flout them. 1106

Every law in Nature, as gravity, centripetence, repulsion, polarity, undulation, has a counterpart in the intellect. The laws above are sisters of the laws below. Shall we study the mathematics of the sphere, and not its causal essence also? Nature is a fable whose moral blazes through it.   1107

Every inch of the mountains is scarred by unimaginable convulsions, yet the new day is purple with the bloom of youth and love.   1108

It happens sometimes that poets do not believe their own poetry; they are so much the less poets.   1109

All vigor is contagious, and when we see creation we also begin to create. Depth of character, height of genius, can only find nourishment in this soil. The miracles of genius always rest on profound convictions which refuse to be analyzed. Enthusiasm is the leaping lightning, not to be measured by the horse-power of the understanding. Hope never spreads her golden wings but on unfathomable seas.   1110

A strenuous soul hates cheap successes. It is the ardor of the assailant that makes the vigor of the defender. The great are not tender at being obscure, despised, insulted. Such only feel themselves in adverse fortune. Strong men greet war, tempest, hard times, which search till they find resistance and bottom.   1111

INSPIRATION

There are times when the intellect is so active that everything seems to run to meet it.   1112

The aboriginal man, in geology and in the dim lights of Darwin's microscope, is not an engaging figure. We are very glad that he ate his fishes and snails and marrow-bones out of our sight and hearing, and that his doleful experiences were got through with so very long ago. They combed his mane, they pared his nails, cut off his tail, set him on end, sent him to school and made him pay taxes, before he could begin to write his sad story for the compassion or the repudiation of his descendants, who are all but unanimous to disown him. We must take him as we find him,—pretty well on in his education, and, in all our knowledge of him, an interesting creature, with a will, an invention, an imagination, a conscience and an inextinguishable hope.   1113

In the savage man, thought is infantile; and, in the civilized, unequal and ranging up and down a long scale.   1114

Everything which we hear for the first time was expected by the mind; the newest discovery was expected. In the mind we call this enlarged power Inspiration. I believe that nothing great and lasting can be done except by inspiration, by leaning on the secret augury.   1115

A rush of thoughts is the only conceivable prosperity that can come to us. Fine clothes, equipages, villa, park, social consideration, cannot cover up real poverty and insignificance, from my own eyes or from others like mine.   1116

Thoughts let us into realities. Neither miracle nor magic nor any religious tradition, not the immortality of the private soul is incredible after we have experienced an insight, a thought. I think it comes to some men but once in their life, sometimes a religious impulse, sometimes an intellectual insight.   1117

What metaphysician has undertaken to enumerate the tonics of the torpid mind, the rules for the recovery of inspiration? That is least within control which is best in them. Of the *modus* of inspiration we have no knowledge. But in the experience of meditative men there is a certain agreement as to the conditions of reception.   1118

There are thoughts beyond the reaches of our souls.   1119

See how the passions augment our force,—anger, love, ambition!—sometimes sympathy, and the expectation of men. Garrick said that on the stage his great paroxysms surprised himself as much as his audience.   1120

Aristotle said: "No great genius was ever without some mixture of madness, nor can anything grand or superior to the voice of common mortals be spoken except by the agitated soul."   1121

A man must be able to escape from his cares and fears, as well as from hunger and want of sleep.   1122

The fine influences of the morning few can explain, but all will admit.   1123

Every artist knows well some favorite retirement.   1124

When the spirit chooses you for its scribe to publish some commandment, it makes you odious to men and men odious to you, and you shall accept that loathsomeness with joy. The moth must fly to the lamp, and you must solve those questions though you die.   1125

· Fact-books, if the facts be well and thoroughly told, are much more nearly allied to poetry than many books that are written in rhyme.   Only our newest knowledge works as a source of inspiration and thought, as only the outmost layer of *liber* on the tree.   1126

All our power, all our happiness consists in our reception of its (the soul's) hints, which ever become clearer and grander as they are obeyed.   1127

GREATNESS

Self-respect is the early form in which greatness appears.
1128

If a man's centrality is incomprehensible to us, we may as well snub the sun.
1129

A sensible man does not brag, avoids introducing the names of his creditable companions, omits himself as habitually as another man obtrudes himself in the discourse, and is content with putting his fact or theme simply on its ground.
1130

A point of education that I can never too much insist upon is this tenet that every individual man has a bias which he must obey, and that it is only as he feels and obeys this that he rightly develops and attains his legitimate power in the world.
1131

It is easy for a commander to command.
1132

Set ten men to write their journal for one day, and nine of them will leave out their thought, or proper result,—that is, their net experience,—and lose themselves in misreporting the supposed experience of other people.
1133

I have observed that in all public speaking, the rule of the orator begins, not in the array of his facts, but when his deep conviction, and the right and necessity he feels to convey that conviction to his audience,—when these shine and burn in his address; when the thought which he stands for gives its own authority to him, adds to him a grander personality, gives him valor, breadth and new intellectual power, so that not he, but mankind, seems to speak through his lips. There is a certain transfiguration; all great orators have it, and men who wish to be orators simulate it.   1134

But if the first rule is to obey your native bias, to accept that work for which you were inwardly formed,—the second rule is concentration, which doubles its force. Thus if you are a scholar, be that. The same laws hold for you as for the laborer. The shoemaker makes a good shoe because he makes nothing else. Let the student mind his own charge; sedulously wait every morning for the news concerning the structure of the world which the spirit will give him.   1135

No way has been found for making heroism easy, even for the scholar. Labor, iron labor, is for him. The world was created as an audience for him; the atoms of which it is made are opportunities.   1136

The day will come when no badge, uniform or medal will be worn; when the eye, which carries in it planetary influences from all the stars, will indicate rank fast enough by exerting power.   1137

Extremes meet, and there is no better example than the haughtiness of humility. No aristocrat, no prince born to the purple, can begin to compare with the self-respect of the saint.
1138

Shall I tell you the secret of the true scholar? It is this: Every man I meet is my master in some point, and in that I learn of him.   1139

Meantime we hate snivelling. I do not wish you to surpass others in any narrow or professional or monkish way. We like the natural greatness of health and wild power.   1140

Wit is a magnet to find wit, and character to find character. Do you not know that people are as those with whom they converse? And if all or any are heavy to me, that fact accuses me.   .   1141

Why complain, as if a man's debt to his inferiors were not at least equal to his debt to his superiors? If men were equals, the waters would not move; but the difference of level which makes Niagara a cataract, makes eloquence, indignation, poetry, in him who finds there is much to communicate.   1142

IMMORTALITY

The credence of men, more than race or climate, makes their manners and customs; and the history of religion may be read in the forms of sepulture. There never was a time when the doctrine of a future life was not held. 1143

As the savage could not detach in his mind the life of the soul from the body, he took great care for his body. Thus the whole life of man in the first ages was ponderously determined on death. 1144

Christianity brought a new wisdom. But learning depends on the learner. No more truth can be conveyed than the popular mind can bear, and the barbarians who received the cross took the doctrine of the resurrection as the Egyptians took it. It was an affair of the body, and narrowed again by the fury of sect; so that grounds were sprinkled with holy water to receive only orthodox dust; and to keep the body still more sacredly safe for resurrection, it was put into the walls of the church; and the churches of Europe are really sepulchres. 1145

The most remarkable step in the religious history of recent ages is that made by the genius of Swedenborg, who described the moral faculties and affections of man, with the hard realism of an astronomer describing the suns and planets of our system, and explained his opinion of the history and destiny of souls in a narrative form, as of one who had gone in a trance into the society of other worlds. 1146

Sufficient to to-day are the duties of to-day. Don't waste life in doubts and fears; spend yourself on the work before you, well assured that the right performance of this hour's duties will be the best preparation for the hours or ages that follow it. 1147

[193]

A man of thought is willing to die, willing to live; I suppose because he has seen the thread on which the beads are strung, and perceived that it reaches up and down, existing quite independently of the present illusions. A man of affairs is afraid to die, is pestered with terrors, because he has not this vision, and is the victim of those who have moulded the religious doctrines into some neat and plausible system, as Calvinism, Romanism or Swedenborgism, for household use. It is the fear of the young bird to trust its wings. The experiences of the soul will fast outgrow this alarm. The saying of Marcus Antoninus it were hard to mend: "It is well to die if there be gods, and sad to live if there be none." 1148

Hear the opinion of Montesquieu: "If the immortality of the soul were an error, I should be sorry not to believe it. I avow that I am not so humble as the atheist; I know not how they think, but for me, I do not wish to exchange the idea of immortality against that of the beatitude of one day. I delight in believing myself as immortal as God himself. Independently of revealed ideas, metaphysical ideas give me a vigorous hope of my eternal well-being, which I would never renounce." 1149

The healthy state of mind is the love of life. What is so good, let it endure. 1150

I admit that you shall find a good deal of skepticism in the streets and hotels and places of coarse amusement. But that is only to say that the practical faculties are faster developed than the spiritual. Where there is depravity there is a slaughter-house style of thinking. One argument of future life is the recoil of the mind in such company,—our pain at every skeptical statement. 1151

Our disgust is the protest of human nature against a lie.
1152

The ground of hope is in the infinity of the world; which infinity reappears in every particle, the powers of all society in every individual, and of all mind in every mind. I know against all appearances that the universe can receive no detriment; that there is a remedy for every wrong and a satisfaction for every soul.   1153

Everything is prospective, and man is to live hereafter. That the world is for his education is the only sane solution of the enigma. And I think that the naturalist works not for himself, but for the believing mind, which turns his discoveries to revelations, receives them as private tokens of the grand good will of the Creator.   1154

All I have seen teaches me to trust the Creator for all I have not seen. Whatever it be which the great Providence prepares for us, it must be something large and generous, and in the great style of his works.   1155

The soul does not age with the body. On the borders of the grave, the wise man looks forward with equal elasticity of mind, or hope.   1156

It is a proverb of the world that good will makes intelligence, that goodness itself is an eye; and the one doctrine in which all religions agree is that new light is added to the mind in proportion as it uses that which it has.   1157

On these grounds I think that wherever man ripens, this audacious belief (in immortality) presently appears,—in the savage, savagely; in the good, purely. As soon as thought is exercised, this belief is inevitable; as soon as virtue glows, this belief confirms itself. It is a kind of summary or completion of man.   1158

We live by desire to live; we live by choice; by will, by thought, by virtue, by the vivacity of the laws which we obey, and, obeying, share their life,—or we die by sloth, by disobedience, by losing hold of life, which ebbs out of us.   1159

I am a better believer, and all serious souls are better believers in the immortality, than we can give grounds for. The real evidence is too subtle, or is higher than we can write down in propositions.   *   *   *   *   We cannot prove our faith by syllogisms.   1160

Not by literature or theology, but only by rare integrity, by a man permeated and perfumed with airs of heaven,—with manliest or womanliest enduring love,—can the vision (of immortality) be clear to a use the most sublime. And hence the fact that in the minds of men the testimony of a few inspired souls has had such weight and penetration.   1161

Jesus explained nothing, but the influence of him took people out of time, and they felt eternal. A great integrity makes us immortal; an admiration, a deep love, a strong will, arms us above fear. It makes a day memorable. We say we lived years in that hour.   1162

Within every man's thought is a higher thought,—within the character he exhibits to-day, a higher character. The youth puts off the illusions of the child, the man puts off the ignorance and tumultuous passions of youth; proceeding thence puts off the egotism of manhood, and becomes at last a public and universal soul. He is rising to greater heights, but also rising to realities; the outer relations and circumstances dying out, he entering deeper into God, God into him, until the last garment of egotism falls, and he is with God,—shares the will and the immensity of the First Cause.   1163

SELF-RELIANCE

Henceforth, please God, forever I forego
The yoke of men's opinions. I will be
Light-hearted as a bird, and live with God.
I find him in the bottom of my heart,
I hear continually his voice therein.   1164

The little needle always knows the North,
The little bird remembereth his note,
And this wise Seer within me never errs.
I never taught it what it teaches me;
I only follow, when I act aright.   1165

ALONE IN ROME

(Written at Rome—1833)

Alone in Rome. Why, Rome is lonely too;—
Besides, you need not be alone; the soul
Shall have society of its own rank.
Be great, be true, and all the Scipios,
The Catos, the wise patriots of Rome,
Shall flock to you and tarry by your side,
And comfort you with their high company.
Virtue alone is sweet society,
It keeps the key to all heroic hearts,
And opens you a welcome in them all.
You must be like them if you desire them,
Scorn trifles and embrace a better aim
Than wine or sleep or praise;
Hunt knowledge as the lover wooes a maid,
And ever in the strife of your own thoughts
Obey the nobler impulse; that is Rome:
That shall command a senate to your side;
For there is no might in the universe
That can contend with love. It reigns forever.   1166

MUSIC

Let me go where'er I will,
I hear a sky-born music still;
It sounds from all things old,
It sounds from all things young,
From all that's fair, from all that's foul,
Peals out a cheerful song.   1167

It is not only in the rose,
It is not only in the bird,
Not only where the rainbow glows,
Nor in the song of woman heard,
But in the darkest, meanest things
There alway, alway something sings.   1168

'Tis not in the high stars alone,
Nor in the cup of budding flowers,
Nor in the redbreast's mellow tone,
Nor in the bow that smiles in showers,
But in the mud and scum of things
There alway, alway something sings.   1169

He builded better than he knew;—
The conscious stone to beauty grew.   1170
                              —*The Problem.*

Nor knowest thou what argument
Thy life to thy neighbor's creed has lent.
All are needed by each one;
Nothing is fair or good alone.   1171
                              —*Each and All.*

By the rude bridge that arched the flood,
    Their flag to April's breeze unfurl'd;
Here once the embattl'd farmers stood,
    And fired the shot heard round the world. 1172
                              —*Concord Hymn.*

ENGLISH TRAITS

ABILITY

These Saxons are the hands of mankind. They have the taste for toil, a distaste for pleasure or repose, and the telescopic appreciation of distant gain. They are the wealth-makers,— and by dint of mental faculty which has its own conditions.
1173

The people have that nervous bilious temperament which is known by medical men to resist every means employed to make its possessor subservient to the will of others.   1174

In the courts the independence of the judges and the loyalty of the suitors are equally excellent. In parliament they have hit on that capital invention of freedom, a constitutional opposition. And when courts and parliament are both deaf, the plaintiff is not silenced. Calm, patient, his weapon of defence from year to year is the obstinate reproduction of the grievance, with calculations and estimates. But, meantime, he is drawing numbers and money to his opinion, resolved that if all remedy fails, right of revolution is at the bottom of his charter-box. They are bound to see their measure carried, and stick to it through ages of defeat.   1175

The bias of the nation is a passion for utility. They love the lever, the screw and pulley, the Flanders draught-horse, the waterfall, windmills, tide-mills; the sea and the wind to bear their freight ships.   1176

The Frenchman invented the ruffle; the Englishman added the shirt.   1177

They have no Indian taste for a tomahawk-dance, no French taste for a badge or a proclamation. The Englishman is peaceably minding his business and earning his day's wages. But if you offer to lay hand on his day's wages, on his cow, or his right in common, or his shop, he will fight to the Judgment. Magna-charta, jury-trial, habeas-corpus, star-chamber, ship-money, Popery, Plymouth colony, American Revolution, are all questions involving a yeoman's right to his dinner, and except as touching that, would not have lashed the British nation to rage and revolt.   1178

Their drowsy minds need to be flagellated by war and trade and politics and persecution. They cannot well read a principle, except by the light of fagots and of burning towns.
                                                                    1179

They have a wealth of men to fill important posts, and the vigilance of party criticism insures the selection of a competent person.   1180

Is it the smallness of the country, or is it the pride and affection of race,—they have solidarity, or responsibleness, and trust in each other.   1181

The very felons have their pride in each other's English stanchness. In politics and in war they hold together as by hooks of steel.   1182

ENGLISH TRAITS

ARISTOCRACY

A susceptible man could not wear a name which represented in a strict sense a city or a county of England, without hearing in it a challenge to duty and honor.   1183

The English go to their estates for grandeur.   The French live at court, and exile themselves to their estates for economy.
1184

For a race yields a nobility in some form, however we name the lords, as surely as it yields women.   1185

You cannot wield great agencies without lending yourself to them, and when it happens that the spirit of the earl meets his rank and duties, we have the best examples of behavior. Power of any kind readily appears in the manners.   1186

These people seem to gain as much as they lose by their position.   They survey society as from the top of St. Paul's, and if they never hear plain truth from men, they see the best of everything, in every kind, and they see things so grouped and amassed as to infer easily the sum and genius, instead of tedious particularities.   Their good behavior deserves all its fame, and they have that simplicity and that air of repose which are the finest ornament of greatness.   1187

The upper classes have only birth, say the people here, and not thoughts. Yes, but they have manners, and it is wonderful how much talent runs into manners;—nowhere and never so much as in England. They have the sense of superiority, the absence of all the ambitious effort which disgusts in the aspiring classes, a pure tone of thought and feeling, and the power to command, among other luxuries, the presence of the most accomplished men in their festive meetings.   1188

Loyalty is in the English a sub-religion. They wear the laws as ornaments, and walk by their faith in their painted May-Fair as if among the forms of gods.   1189

Politeness is the ritual of society, as prayers are of the church, a school of manners, and a gentle blessing to the age in which it grew. 'Tis a romance adorning English life with a larger horizon; a midway heaven, fulfilling to their sense their fairy tales and poetry.   1190

On general grounds, whatever tends to form manners or to finish men, has a great value. Every one who has tasted the delight of friendship will respect every social guard which our manners can establish, tending to secure from the intrusion of frivolous and distasteful people. The jealousy of every class to guard itself is a testimony to the reality they have found in life. When a man once knows that he has done justice to himself, let him dismiss all terrors of aristocracy as superstitions, so far as he is concerned.   1191

Everybody who is real is open and ready for that which is also real.   1192

Every victory was the defeat of a party only less worthy.
1193

A multitude of English, educated at the universities, bred into their society with manners, ability and the gifts of fortune, are every day confronting the peers on a footing of equality, and outstripping them, as often, in the race of honor and influence. ** They cannot shut their eyes to the fact that an untitled nobility possess all the power without the inconveniences that belong to rank.   1194

ENGLISH TRAITS
CHARACTER

Their habits and instincts cleave to nature. They are of the earth, earthy; and of the sea, as the sea-kinds, attached to it for what it yields them, and not from any sentiment. They are full of coarse strength, rude exercise, butcher's meat and sound sleep; and suspect any poetic insinuation or any hint for the conduct of life which reflects on this animal existence.   1195

There are multitudes of rude young English who have the self-sufficiency and bluntness of their nation, and who, with their disdain of the rest of mankind and with this indigestion and choler, have made the English traveller a proverb for uncomfortable and offensive manners.   1196

They dare to displease, they do not speak to expectation. They like the sayers of No, better than the sayers of Yes.   1197

More intellectual than other races, when they live with other races they do not take their language, but bestow their own. They subsidize other nations, and are not subsidized. They proselyte, and are not proselyted. They assimilate other races to themselves, and are not assimilated. The English did not calculate the conquest of the Indies. It fell to their character.
                                                                 1198

Our swifter Americans, when they first deal with English, pronounce them stupid; but, later, do them justice as people who wear well, or hide their strength.   1199

The national temper, in the civil history, is not flashy or whiffling. The slow, deep English mass smoulders with fire, which at last sets all its borders in flame. The wrath of London is not French wrath, but has a long memory, and, in its hottest heat, a register and rule.   1200

The stability of England is the security of the modern world.
                                                        1201

They wish neither to command nor obey, but to be kings in their own houses.   1202

ENGLISH TRAITS

COCKAYNE (Imaginary Luxury)

There is no freak so ridiculous but some Englishman has attempted to immortalize by money and law.   1203

The English have a steady courage that fits them for great attempts and endurance; they have also a petty courage, through which every man delights in showing himself for what he is and in doing what he can; so that in all companies, each of them has too good an opinion of himself to imitate anybody. He hides no defect of his form, features, dress, connection, or birthplace, for he thinks every circumstance belonging to him comes recommended to you.   1204

A man's personal defects will commonly have, with the rest of the world, precisely that importance which they have to himself. If he makes light of them, so will other men.   1205

An English lady on the Rhine, hearing a German speaking of her party as foreigners, exclaimed, "No, we are not foreigners; we are English; it is you that are foreigners."   1206

The English dislike the American structure of society, whilst yet trade, mills, public education and Chartism are doing what they can to create in England the same social condition.   1207

Nature and destiny are always on the watch for our follies. Nature trips us up when we strut.   1208

ENGLISH TRAITS

LITERATURE

A strong common sense, which it is not easy to unseat or disturb, marks the English mind for a thousand years. 1209

When he is intellectual, and a poet or a philosopher, he carries the same hard truth and the same keen machinery into the mental sphere. His mind must stand on a fact. He will not be baffled, or catch at clouds, but the mind must have a symbol palpable and resisting. 1210

Byron "liked something craggy to break his mind upon." 1211

To the images from this twin source (of Christianity and art), the mind became fruitful as by the incubation of the Holy Ghost. The English mind flowered in every faculty. The common sense was surprised and inspired. For two centuries England was philosophic, religious, poetic. The mental furniture seemed of larger scale; the memory capacious like the storehouse of the rains. The ardor and endurance of study, the boldness and facility of their mental construction, their fancy and imagination and easy spanning of vast distances of thought, the enterprise or accosting of new subjects, and, generally, the easy exertion of power,—astonish, like the legendary feats of Guy of Warwick. 1212

Their dynamic brains hurled off their words as the revolving stone hurls off scraps of grit. I could cite from the seventeenth century sentences and phrases of edge not to be matched in the nineteenth. 1213

Judge of the splendor of a nation by the insignificance of
great individuals in it.   1214

The influence of Plato tinges the British genius.   Their
minds loved analogy; were cognizant of resemblances, and
climbers on the staircase of unity.   1215

Whoever discredits analogy and requires heaps of facts before
any theories can be attempted, has no poetic power, and nothing
original or beautiful will be produced by him.   1216

A few generalizations always circulate in the world, whose
authors we do not rightly know, which astonish, and appear
to be avenues to vast kingdoms of thought, and these are in
the world *constants*, like the Copernican and Newtonian theories in physics.   1217

Hallam is uniformly polite, but with deficient sympathy;
writes with resolute generosity, but is unconscious of the deep
worth which lies in the mystics, and which often outvalues as
a seed of power and a source of revolution all the correct
writers and shining reputations of their day.   He passes in
silence, or dismisses with a kind of contempt, the profounder
masters; a lover of ideas is not only uncongenial, but
unintelligible.   1218

It is very certain *** that if Lord Bacon had been only
the sensualist his critic pretends, he would never have acquired
the fame which now entitles him to this patronage.   It is
because he had imagination, the leisures of the spirit, and basked
in an element of contemplation out of all modern English
atmospheric gauges, that he is impressive to the imaginations
of men and has become a potentate not to be ignored.   1219

The necessities of mental structure force all minds into a few
categories; and where impatience of the tricks of men makes
Nemesis amiable, and builds altars to the negative Deity, the
inevitable recoil is to heroism or the gallantry of the private
heart, which decks its immolation with glory, in the unequal
combat of will against fate.   1220

The bias of Englishmen to practical skill has reacted on the
national mind.   They are incapable of an inutility, and respect
the five mechanic powers even in their song.   The voice of their
modern muse has a slight hint of the steam-whistle, and the
poem is created as an ornament and finish of their monarchy,
and by no means as the bird of a new morning which forgets
the past world in the full enjoyment of that which is forming.
                                                         1221

A good Englishman shuts himself out of three fourths of
his mind and confines himself to one fourth.   1222

But English science puts humanity to the door.   It wants
the connection which is the test of genius.   The science is false
by not being poetic.   It isolates the reptile or mollusk it
assumes to explain; whilst reptile or mollusk only exists in
system, in relation.   The poet only sees it as an inevitable step
in the path of the Creator.   1223

Meantime, I know that a retrieving power lies in the English race which seems to make any recoil possible; in other words, there is at all times a minority of profound minds existing in the nation, capable of appreciating every soaring of intellect and every hint of tendency. While the constructive talent seems dwarfed and superficial, the criticism is often in the noblest tone and suggests the presence of the invisible gods.   1224

ENGLISH TRAITS
MANCHESTER SPEECH

I have not the smallest interest in any holiday except as it celebrates real and not pretended joys.   1225

For I must tell you, I was given to understand in my childhood that the British island from which my forefathers came was no lotus-garden, no paradise of serene sky and roses and music and merriment all the year round, no, but a cold, foggy, mournful country, where nothing grew well in the open air but robust men and virtuous women, and these of a wonderful fibre and endurance; that their best parts were slowly revealed; their virtues did not come out until they quarrelled; they did not strike twelve the first time; good lovers, good haters, and you could know little about them till you had seen them long, and little good of them till you had seen them in action; that in prosperity they were moody and dumpish, but in adversity they were grand.   1226

Seeing this, I say, All hail! mother of nations, mother of heroes, with strength still equal to the time; still wise to entertain and swift to execute the policy which the mind and heart of mankind requires in the present hour, and thus only hospitable to the foreigner and truly a home to the thoughtful and generous who are born in the soil.   1227

ENGLISH TRAITS
MANNERS

I find the Englishman to be him of all men who stands firmest in his shoes.   1228

They require you to dare to be of your own opinion, and they hate the practical cowards who cannot in affairs answer directly yes or no. They dare to displease, nay, they will let you break all the commandments, if you do it natively and with spirit. You must be somebody; then you may do this or that, as you will.   1229

The Englishman speaks with all his body. His elocution is stomachic,—as the American's is labial.   1230

A Frenchman may possibly be clean; an Englishman is conscientiously clean.   1231

Every Englishman is an embryonic chancellor; his instinct is to search for a precedent. The favorite phrase of their law is, "a custom whereof the memory of man runneth not back to the contrary." ** They hate innovation.   1232

ENGLISH TRAITS
RACE

Each religious sect has its physiognomy. The Methodists have acquired a face; the Quakers, a face; the nuns, a face. An Englishman will pick out a dissenter by his manners. Trades and professions carve their own lines on face and form.   1233

The best nations are those most widely related; and navigation, as effecting a world-wide mixture, is the most potent advancer of nations.   1234

I incline to the belief that, as water, lime and sand make mortar, so certain temperaments marry well, and, by well-managed contrarieties, develop as drastic a character as the English.   1235

Perhaps the ocean serves as a galvanic battery, to distribute acids at one pole and alkalies at the other. So England tends to accumulate her liberals in America, and her conservatives at London.   1236

It is a medical fact that the children of the blind see; the children of felons have a healthy conscience.   1237

The French say that the Englishwomen have two left hands.   1238

As soon as he can handle a gun, hunting is the fine art of every Englishman of condition. They are the most voracious people of prey that ever existed. Every season turns out the aristocracy into the country to shoot and fish. The more vigorous run out of the island to America, to Asia, to Africa and Australia, to hunt with fury by gun, by trap, by harpoon, by lasso, with dog, with horse, with elephant or with dromedary, all the game that is in nature. These men have written the game-books of all countries, as Hawker, Scrope, Murray, Herbert, Maxwell, Cumming and a host of travellers. The people at home are addicted to boxing, running, leaping and rowing matches.   1239

Men of animal nature rely, like animals, on their instincts. The Englishman associates well with dogs and horses. His attachment to the horse arises from the courage and address required to manage it. The horse finds out who is afraid of it, and does not disguise its opinion. Their young boiling clerks and lusty collegians like the company of horses better than the company of professors. I suppose the horses are better company for them.   1240

It is a proverb in England that it is safer to shoot a man than a hare. The severity of the game-laws certainly indicates an extravagant sympathy of the nation with horses and hunters.
                                                        1241

ENGLISH TRAITS
RELIGION

It is with religion as with marriage. A youth marries in haste; afterwards, when his mind is opened to the reason of the conduct of life, he is asked what he thinks of the institution of marriage and of the right relations of the sexes? "I should have much to say," he might reply, "if the question were open, but I have a wife and children, and all question is closed for me."   1242

England felt the full heat of the Christianity which fermented Europe, and drew, like the chemistry of fire, a firm line between barbarism and culture. The power of the religious sentiment put an end to human sacrifices, checked appetite, inspired the crusades, inspired resistance to tyrants, inspired self-respect, set bounds to serfdom and slavery, founded liberty, created the religious architecture.   1243

The English Church has many certificates to show of humble effective service in humanizing the people, in cheering and refining men, feeding, healing and educating. It has the seal of martyrs and confessors; the noblest books; a sublime architecture; a ritual marked by the same secular merits, nothing cheap or purchasable.   1244

The reverence for the Scriptures is an element of civilization, for thus has the history of the world been preserved and is preserved.   1245

From his infancy, every Englishman is accustomed to hear daily prayers for the Queen, for the royal family and the Parliament, by name; and this lifelong consecration cannot be without influence on his opinions.   1246

Good churches are not built by bad men; at least there must be probity and enthusiasm somewhere in the society. These minsters were neither built nor filled by atheists.   1247

Heats and genial periods arrive in history, or, shall we say, plenitudes of Divine Presence, by which high tides are caused in the human spirit, and great virtues and talents appear, as in the eleventh, twelfth, thirteenth, and again in the sixteenth and seventeenth centuries, when the nation was full of genius and piety.   1248

The spirit that dwelt in this church has glided away to animate other activities, and they who come to the old shrines find apes and players rustling the old garments.   1249

The torpidity on the side of religion of the vigorous English understanding shows how much wit and folly can agree in one brain.   Their religion is a quotation; their church is a doll; and any examination is interdicted with screams of terror.   In good company you expect them to laugh at the fanaticism of the vulgar; but they do not; they are the vulgar.   1250

Where dwells the religion?   Tell me first where dwells electricity, or motion, or thought, or gesture.   They do not dwell or stay at all.   Electricity cannot be made fast, mortared up and ended, like London Monument or the Tower, so that you shall know where to find it, and keep it fixed, as the English do with their things, forevermore; it is passing, glancing, gesticular; it is a traveller, a newness, a surprise, a secret, which perplexes them and puts them out.   1251

ENGLISH TRAITS

THE TIMES NEWSPAPER

The most conspicuous result of this talent is the Times newspaper. No power in England is more felt, more feared, or more obeyed. What you read in the morning in that journal, you shall hear in the evening in all society. It has ears everywhere, and its information is earliest, completest and surest. It has risen, year by year, and victory by victory, to its present authority. 1252

The statistics are now quite out of date, but I remember he told us that the daily printing was then 35,000 copies; that on the 1st March, 1848, the greatest number ever printed—54,000—were issued. 1253

"What would The Times say?" is a terror in Paris, in Berlin, in Vienna, in Copenhagen and in Nepaul. Its consummate discretion and success exhibit the English skill of combination. 1254

There is always safety in valor. 1255

It is usually pretended, in Parliament and elsewhere, that the English press has a high tone,—which it has not. It has an imperial tone, as of a powerful and independent nation. 1256

ENGLISH TRAITS

TRUTH

The German name has a proverbial significance of sincerity and honest meaning. The arts bear testimony to it. The faces of the clergy and laity in old sculptures and illuminated missals are charged with earnest belief. Add to this hereditary rectitude the punctuality and precise dealing which commerce creates, and you have the English truth and credit.   1257

Beasts that make no truce with man, do not break faith with each other. 'Tis said that the wolf, who makes a *cache* of his prey and brings his fellows with him to the spot, if, on digging, it is not found, is instantly and unresistingly torn in pieces.   1258

They confide in each other,—English believes in English. The French feel the superiority of this probity. The Englishman is not springing a trap for his admiration, but is honestly minding his business. The Frenchman is vain. Madame de Stael says that the English irritated Napoleon, mainly because they have found out how to unite success with honesty.   1259

The ruling passion of Englishmen in these days is a terror of humbug. In the same proportion they value honesty, stoutness, and adherence to your own. They like a man committed to his objects. They hate the French, as frivolous; they hate the Irish, as aimless; they hate the Germans, as professors.
1260

English stolidity contrasts with French wit and tact. The French, it is commonly said, have greatly more influence in Europe than the English. What influence the English have is by brute force of wealth and power; that of the French by affinity and talent. The Italian is subtle, the Spaniard treacherous; tortures, it is said, could never wrest from an Egyptian the confession of a secret.   1261

ENGLISH TRAITS
UNIVERSITIES

It is contended by those who have been bred at Eton, Harrow, Rugby and Westminster, that the public sentiment within each of those schools is high-toned and manly; that, in their playgrounds, courage is universally admired, meanness despised, manly feelings and generous conduct are encouraged; that an unwritten code of honor deals to the spoiled child of rank and to the child of upstart wealth, an even-handed justice, purges their nonsense out of both and does all that can be done to make them gentlemen.   1262

Again, the great number of cultivated men keep each other up to a high standard. The habit of meeting well-read and knowing men teaches the art of omission and selection.   1263

Universities are of course hostile to geniuses, which, seeing and using ways of their own, discredit the routine; as churches and monasteries persecute youthful saints.   1264

England is the land of mixture and surprise, and when you have settled it that the universities are moribund, out comes a poetic influence from the heart of Oxford, to mould the opinions of cities, to build their houses as simply as birds their nests, to give veracity to art and charm mankind, as an appeal to moral order always must.   But besides this restorative genius, the best poetry of England of this age, in the old forms, comes from two graduates at Cambridge.   (Wordsworth and Byron.)
1265

ENGLISH TRAITS

First Visit to England in 1833

Wordsworth honored himself by his simple adherence to truth, and was very willing not to shine; but he surprised by the hard limits of his thought. To judge from a single conversation, he made the impression of a narrow and very English mind; of one who paid for his rare elevation by general tameness and conformity. Off his own beat, his opinions were of no value. It is not very rare to find persons loving sympathy and ease, who expiate their departure from the common in one direction, by their conformity in every other.   1266

Voyage to England in 1847

A great mind is a good sailor, as a great heart is. And the sea is not slow in disclosing inestimable secrets to a good naturalist.   1267

The busiest talk with leisure and convenience at sea.   1268

Under the best conditions, a voyage is one of the severest tests to try a man. A college examination is nothing to it.   1269

ENGLISH TRAITS

WEALTH

The respect for truth of facts in England is equalled only by the respect for wealth. It is at once the pride of art of the Saxon, as he is a wealth-maker, and his passion for independence. The Englishman believes that every man must take care of himself, and has himself to thank if he do not mend his condition. To pay their debts is their national point of honor. 1270

The house is a castle which the king cannot enter. The Bank is a strong box to which the king has no key. Whatever surly sweetness possession can give, is tasted in England to the dregs. Vested rights are awful things, and absolute possession gives the smallest freeholder identity of interest with the duke. High stone fences and padlocked garden-gates announce the absolute will of the owner to be alone. Every whim of exaggerated egotism is put into stone and iron, into silver and gold, with costly deliberation and detail. 1271

But it is found that the machine unmans the user. What he gains in making cloth, he loses in general power. * * * The incessant repetition of the same hand-work dwarfs the man, robs him of his strength, wit and versatility, to make a pin-polisher, a buckle-maker, or any other specialty. 1272

We estimate the wisdom of nations by seeing what they did with their surplus capital. 1273

DEMONOLOGY

The witchcraft of sleep divides with truth the empire of our lives.   1274

Dreams have a poetic integrity and truth. This limbo and dust-hole of thought is presided over by a certain reason, too. Their extravagance from nature is yet within a higher nature. They seem to us to suggest an abundance and fluency of thought not familiar to the waking experience.   1275

Wise and sometimes terrible hints shall in them (dreams) be thrown to the man out of a quite unknown intelligence.
1276

We are let by this experience into the high region of Cause, and acquainted with the identity of very unlike-seeming effects.
1277

The soul contains in itself the event that shall presently befall it, for the event is only the actualizing of its thoughts.
1278

Every man goes through the world attended with innumerable facts prefiguring (yes, distinctly announcing) his fate, if only eyes of sufficient heed and illumination were fastened on the sign.   1279

All life, all creation, is telltale and betraying. A man reveals himself in every glance and step and movement and rest.   1280

Not a mathematical axiom but is a moral rule. The jest and byword to an intelligent ear extends its meaning to the soul and to all time.   1281

One moment of a man's life is a fact so stupendous as to take the lustre out of all fiction.___   1282

It (Demonology) is a midsummer madness, corrupting all who hold the tenet. The demonologic is only a fine name for egotism; an exaggeration namely of the individual, whom it is Nature's settled purpose to postpone.   1283

Dreams retain the infirmities of our character. The good genius may be there or not, our evil genius is sure to stay.   1284

The history of man is a series of conspiracies to win from Nature some advantage without paying for it. It is curious to see what grand powers we have a hint of and are mad to grasp, yet how slow Heaven is to trust us with such edge-tools.   1285

Before we acquire great power we must acquire wisdom to use it well. Animal magnetism inspires the prudent and moral with a certain terror; so the divination of contingent events, and the alleged second-sight of the pseudo-spiritualists. There are many things of which a wise man might wish to be ignorant, and these are such. Shun them as you would the secrets of the undertaker and the butcher. The best are never demoniacal or magnetic; leave this limbo to the Prince of the power of the air. The lowest angel is better. It is the height of the animal; below the region of the divine. Power as such is not known to the angels.   1286

But as Nature can never be outwitted, as in the Universe no man was ever known to get a cent's worth without paying in some form or other the cent, so this prodigious promiser ends always and always will, as sorcery and alchemy have done before, in very small and smoky performance.   1287

The whole world is an omen and a sign. Why look so
wistfully in a corner? Man is the Image of God. Why run
after a ghost or a dream? The voice of divination resounds
everywhere and runs to waste unheard, unregarded, as the
mountains echo with the bleatings of cattle.   1288

ARISTOCRACY

Every man confesses that the highest good which the universe proposes to him is the highest society.   1289

The game of the world is a perpetual trial of strength between man and events.   The common man is the victim of events.   1290

Men of aim must lead the aimless; men of invention the uninventive.   I wish catholic men, who by their science and skill are at home in every latitude and longitude, who carry the world in their thoughts; men of universal politics, who are interested in things in proportion to their truth and magnitude; who know the beauty of animals and the laws of their nature, whom the mystery of botany allures, and the mineral laws; who see general effects and are not too learned to love the Imagination, the power and the spirits of Solitude;—men who see the dance in men's lives as well as in a ball-room, and can feel and convey the sense which is only collectively or totally expressed by a population; men who are charmed by the beautiful Nemesis as well as by the dire Nemesis, and dare trust their inspiration for their welcome; who would find their fellows in persons of real elevation of whatever kind of speculative or practical ability.   1291

In the heroic ages, as we call them, the hero uniformly has some real talent.   1292

In a thousand cups of life, only one is the right mixture,— a fine adjustment to the existing elements.   1293

An aristocracy could not exist unless it were organic.   Men are born to command.   1294

We pass for what we are, and we prosper or fail by what we are. There are men who may dare much and will be justified in their daring. But it is because they know they are in their place. As long as I am in my place, I am safe. "The best lightning-rod for your protection is your own spine." Let a man's social aims be proportioned to his means and power. I do not pity the misery of a man underplaced; that will right itself presently; but I pity the man overplaced.   1295

A certain quantity of power belongs to a certain quantity of faculty. Whoever wants more power than is the legitimate attraction of his faculty, is a politician, and must pay for that excess.   1296

It will be agreed everywhere that society must have the benefit of the best leaders.   1297

The verdict of battles will best prove the general; the town-meeting, the Congress, will not fail to find out legislative talent. The prerogatives of a right physician are determined, not by his diplomas, but by the health he restores to body and mind; the powers of a geometer by solving his problem; of a priest by the act of inspiring us with a sentiment which disperses the grief from which we suffered. When the lawyer tries his case in court he himself is also on trial and his own merits appear as well as his client's.   1298

What is it that makes the true knight? Loyalty to his thought. That makes the beautiful scorn, the elegant simplicity, the directness, the commanding port which all men admire and which men not noble affect.   1299

The nearer my friend, the more spacious is our realm, the more diameter our spheres have.   1300

The true aristocrat is he who is at the head of his own order, and disloyalty is to mistake other chivalries for his own.   1301

In horsemanship he is not the good rider who never was thrown, but rather that a man never will be a good rider until he is thrown.   1302

In the hours of insight we rally against this skepticism. We then see that if the ignorant are around us, the great are much more near; that there is an order of men, never quite absent, who enroll no names in their archives but of such as are capable of truth.   They are gathered in no one chamber; no chamber would hold them; but, out of the vast duration of man's race, they tower like mountains, and are present to every mind in proportion to its likeness to theirs.   The solitariest man who shares their spirit walks environed by them; they talk to him, they comfort him, and happy is he who prefers these associates to profane companions.   1303

That highest good of rational existence is always coming to such as reject mean alliances.   1304

To every gentleman grave and dangerous duties are proposed. Justice always wants champions.   The world waits for him as its defender, for he will find in the well-dressed crowd, yes, in the civility of whole nations, vulgarity of sentiment.   In the best parlors of modern society he will find the laughing devil, the civil sneer.   1305

Virtue and genius are always on the direct way to the control of the society in which they are found.   It is the interest of society that good men should govern, and there is always a tendency so to place them.   1306

I do not know whether that word Gentleman, although it signifies a leading idea in recent civilization, is a sufficiently broad generalization to convey the deep and grave fact of self-reliance. To many the word expresses only the outsides of cultivated men,—only graceful manners, and independence in trifles; but the fountains of that thought are in the deeps of man, a beauty which reaches through and through, from the manners to the soul; an honor which is only a name for sanctity, a self-trust which is a trust in God himself. Call it man of honor, or call it Man, the American who would serve his country must learn the beauty and honor of perseverance, he must reinforce himself by the power of character, and revisit the margin of that well from which his fathers drew waters of life and enthusiasm, the fountain I mean of the moral sentiments, the parent fountain from which this goodly Universe flows as a wave.   1307

PERPETUAL FORCES

Intellect and morals appear only the material forces on a higher plane. The laws of material nature run up into the invisible world of the mind, and hereby we acquire a key to those sublimities which skulk and hide in the caverns of human consciousness.   1308

We define Genius to be a sensibility to all the impressions of the outer world, a sensibility so equal that it receives accurately all impressions, and can truly report them, without excess or loss, as it received.   1309

The health of man is an equality of inlet and outlet, gathering and giving. Any hoarding is tumor and disease.   1310

The power of persistence, of enduring defeat and of gaining victory by defeats, is one of these forces which never loses its charm.   1311

The last revelation of intellect and of sentiment is that in a manner it severs the man from all other men; makes known to him that the spiritual powers are sufficient to him if no other being existed; that he is to deal absolutely in the world, as if he alone were a system and a state, and though all should perish could make all anew.   1312

Obedience alone gives the right to command. It is like the village operator who taps the telegraph-wire and surprises the secrets of empires as they pass to the capital. So this child of the dust throws himself by obedience into the circuit of the heavenly wisdom, and shares the secret of God.   1313

This world belongs to the energetical.   1314

Things are saturated with the moral law. There is no
escape from it. Violets and grass preach it; rain and snow,
wind and tides, every change, every cause in Nature is nothing
but a disguised missionary.   1315

The illusion that strikes me as the masterpiece in that ring
of illusions which our life is, is the timidity with which we
assert our moral sentiment. We are made of it, the world is
built by it, things endure as they share it; all beauty, all health,
all intelligence exist by it; yet we shrink to speak of it or to
range ourselves by its side. Nay, we presume strength of him
or them who deny it. Cities go against it; the college goes
against it, the courts snatch at any precedent, at any vicious
form of law to rule it out; legislatures listen with appetite to
declamations against it, and vote it down. Every new asserter
of the right surprises us, like a man joining the church, and we
hardly dare believe he is in earnest.   1316

Whence does the knowledge come? Where is the source
of power? The soul of God is poured into the world through
the thoughts of men.   1317

CHARACTER

Morals respects what men call goodness, that which all men agree to honor as justice, truth-speaking, good will and good works. Morals respects the source or motive of this action. It is the science of substances, not of shows. It is the *what*, and not the *how*. It is that which all men profess to regard, and by their real respect for which recommend themselves to each other.   1318

It were an unspeakable calamity if any one should think he had the right to impose a private will on others. That is the part of a striker, an assassin.   1319

Morals is the direction of the will on universal ends.   1320

All the virtues are special directions of this motive; justice is the application of this good of the whole to the affairs of each one; courage is contempt of danger in the determination to see this good of the whole enacted.   1321

On the perpetual conflict between the dictate of this universal mind and the wishes and interests of the individual, the moral discipline of life is built.   1322

He that speaks the truth executes no private function of an individual will, but the world utters a sound by his lips.
1323

The excellence of Jesus, and of every true teacher, is, that he affirms the Divinity in him and in us,—not thrusts himself between it and us.   1324

It happens now and then, in the ages, that a soul is born which has no weakness of self, which offers no impediment to the Divine Spirit, which comes down into Nature as if only for the benefit of souls, and all its thoughts are perceptions of things as they are, without any infirmity of earth. Such souls are as the apparition of gods among men, and simply by their presence pass judgment on them. Men are forced by their own self-respect to give them a certain attention. Evil men shrink and pay involuntary homage by hiding or apologizing for their action.   1325

When a man is born with a profound moral sentiment, preferring truth, justice and the serving of all men to any honors or any gain, men readily feel the superiority. They who deal with him are elevated with joy and hope; he lights up the house or the landscape in which he stands. His actions are poetic and miraculous in their eyes. In his presence, or within his influence, every one believes in the immortality of the soul.   1326

The establishment of Christianity in the world does not rest on any miracle but the miracle of being the broadest and most humane doctrine. Christianity was once a schism and protest against the impieties of the time, which had originally been protests against earlier impieties, but had lost their truth.
                                                             1327

Fifty or a hundred years ago, prayers were said, morning and evening, in all families; grace was said at table; an exact observance of the Sunday was kept in the houses of laymen as of clergymen. And one sees with some pain the disuse of rites so charged with humanity and aspiration. But it by no means follows, because those offices are much disused, that the men and women are irreligious; certainly not that they have less integrity or sentiment, but only, let us hope, that they see that they can omit the form without loss of real ground; perhaps that they find some violence, some cramping of their freedom of thought, in the constant recurrence of the form.   1328

I consider theology to be the rhetoric of morals. The mind of this age has fallen away from theology to morals. I conceive it an advance.   1329

A completed nation will not import its religion.   1330

Our religion has got on as far as Unitarianism. But all the forms grow pale. The walls of the temple are wasted and thin, and, at last, only a film of whitewash, because the mind of our culture has already left our liturgies behind. "Every age," says Varnhagen, "has another sieve for the religious tradition, and will sift it out again. Something is continually lost by this treatment, which posterity cannot recover." 1331

I am far from accepting the opinion that the revelations of the moral sentiment are insufficient, as if it furnished a rule only, and not the spirit by which the rule is animated. 1332

There will always be a class of imaginative youths, whom poetry, whom the love of beauty, lead to the adoration of the moral sentiment, and these will provide it with new historic forms and songs.   1333

Character is the habit of action from the permanent vision of truth. It carries a superiority to all the accidents of life. It compels right relation to every other man,—domesticates itself with strangers and enemies.   1334

EDUCATION

As every wind draws music out of the Æolian harp, so doth every object in Nature draw music out of his mind.
1335

In some sort the end of life is that the man should take up the universe into himself, or out of that quarry leave nothing unrepresented. Yonder mountain must migrate into his mind. Yonder magnificent astronomy he is at last to import, fetching away moon, and planet, solstice, period, comet and binal star, by comprehending their relation and law.
1336

The great object of Education should be commensurate with the object of life. It should be a moral one; to teach self-trust; to inspire the youthful man with an interest in himself; with a curiosity touching his own nature; to acquaint him with the resources of his mind, and to teach him that there is all his strength, and to inflame him with a piety towards the Grand Mind in which he lives. Thus would education conspire with the Divine Providence.
1337

Heaven often protects valuable souls charged with great secrets, great ideas, by long shutting them up with their own thoughts. And the most genial and amiable of men must alternate society with solitude, and learn its severe lessons.
1338

Every mind should be allowed to make its own statement in action, and its balance will appear.
1339

I advise teachers to cherish mother-wit. I assume that you will keep the grammar, reading, writing and arithmetic in order; 'tis easy and of course you will. But smuggle in a little contraband wit, fancy, imagination, thought.
1340

[236]

Consent yourself to be an organ of your highest thought, and lo! suddenly you put all men in your debt, and are the fountain of an energy that goes pulsing on with waves of benefit to the borders of society, to the circumference of things.

1341

THE SUPERLATIVE

Bad news is always exaggerated, and we may challenge Providence to send a fact so tragical that we cannot contrive to make it a little worse in our gossip.   1342

I hear without sympathy the complaint of young and ardent persons that they find life no region of romance, with no enchanter, no giant, no fairies, nor even muses.   1343

Men of the world value truth, in proportion to their ability; not by its sacredness, but for its convenience.   1344

The superlative is the excess of expression.   1345

The expressors are the gods of the world, but the men whom these expressors revere are the solid, balanced, undemonstrative citizens, who make the reserved guard, the central sense, of the world.   1346

Nature is always serious,—does not jest with us.   1347

The men whom she (Nature) admits to her confidence, the simple and great characters, are uniformly marked by absence of pretension.   1348

THE SOVEREIGNTY OF ETHICS

In ignorant ages it was common to vaunt the human superiority by underrating the instinct of other animals; but a better discernment finds that the difference is only of less and more. Experiment shows that the bird and the dog reason as the hunter does, that all the animals show the same good sense in their humble walk that the man who is their enemy or friend does. 1349

The moral is the measure of health, and in the voice of Genius I hear invariably the moral tone, even when it is disowned in words. 1350

The finer the sense of justice, the better poet. 1351

The geologic world is chronicled by the growing ripeness of the strata from lower to higher, as it becomes the abode of more highly-organized plants and animals. The civil history of men might be traced by the successive meliorations as marked in higher moral generalizations;—virtue meaning physical courage, then chastity and temperance, then justice and love; —bargains of kings with peoples of certain rights to certain classes, then of rights to masses,—then at last came the day when, as the historians rightly tell, the nerves of the world were electrified by the proclamation that all men are born free and equal. 1352

In the court of law the judge sits over the culprit, but in the court of life in the same hour the judge also stands as culprit before a true tribunal. Every judge is a culprit, every law an abuse. 1353

The cruelest foe is a masked benefactor.   The wars which make history so dreary have served the cause of truth and virtue.   1354

We are to know that we are never without a pilot.   When we know not how to steer, and dare not hoist a sail, we can drift.   The current knows the way, though we do not.   1355

Virtue is the adopting of this dictate of the universal mind by the individual will.   Character is the habit of this obedience, and Religion is the accompanying emotion, the emotion of reverence which the presence of the universal mind ever excites in the individual.   1356

Worship is the regard for what is above us.   Men are respectable only as they respect.   We delight in children because of that religious eye which belongs to them; because of their reverence for their seniors, and for their objects of belief.
                                                                                        1357

THE PREACHER

But religion has an object. It does not grow thin or robust with the health of the votary. The object of adoration remains forever unhurt and identical. We are in transition, from the worship of the fathers which enshrined the law in a private personal history, to a worship which recognizes the true eternity of the law, its presence to you and me, its equal energy in what is called brute nature as in what is called sacred. The next age will behold God in the ethical laws—as mankind begins to see them in this age, self-equal, self-executing, instantaneous and self-affirmed; needing no voucher, no prophet and no miracle besides their own irresistibility,—and will regard natural history, private fortunes and politics, not for themselves, as we have done, but as illustrations of those laws, of that beatitude and love. 1358

I find myself always struck and stimulated by a good anecdote, any trait of heroism, of faithful service. 1359

All that we call religion, all that saints and churches and Bibles from the beginning of the world have aimed at, is to suppress this impertinent surface-action, and animate man to central and entire action. The human race are afflicted with a St. Vitus's dance; their fingers and toes, their members, their senses, their talents, are superfluously active, while the torpid heart gives no oracle. When that wakes, it will revolutionize the world. 1360

All positive rules, ceremonial, ecclesiastical, distinctions of race or of person, are perishable; only those distinctions hold which are, in the nature of things, not matters of positive ordinance. As the earth we stand upon is not imperishable, but is chemically resolvable into gases and nebulæ, so is the universe an infinite series of planes, each of which is a false bottom; and when we think our feet are planted now at last on adamant, the slide is drawn out from under us.   1361

We come to church properly for self-examination, for approach to principles to see how it stands with *us*, with the deep and dear facts of right and love.   1362

THE SCHOLAR

An Oration Delivered Before the Washington and Jefferson Societies at the University of Virginia, 28th of June, 1876

Every natural power exhilarates; a true talent delights the possessor first. A celebrated musician was wont to say, that men knew not how much more he delighted himself with his playing than he did others.   1363

The scholar is here to fill others with love and courage by confirming their trust in the love and wisdom which are at the heart of all things; to affirm noble sentiments; to hear them wherever spoken, out of the deeps of ages, out of the obscurities of barbarous life, and to republish them;—to untune nobody, but to draw all men after the truth, and to keep men spiritual and sweet.   1364

Language can hardly exaggerate the beatitude of the intellect flowing into the faculties.   1365

Intellect is the science of metes and bounds; yet it sees no bound to the eternal proceeding of law forth into nature. All the sciences are only new applications, each translatable into the other, of the one law which his mind is.   1366

The poet writes his verse on a scrap of paper, and instantly the desire and love of all mankind take charge of it, as if it were Holy Writ.   1367

Man is a torch borne in the wind.   1368

The scholar then is unfurnished who has only literary
weapons.   1369

I invite you not to cheap joys, to the flutter of gratified
vanity, to a sleek and rosy comfort; no, but to bareness, to
power, to enthusiasm, to the mountain of vision, to true and
natural supremacy, to the society of the great, and to love.
Give me bareness and poverty so that I know them as the
sure heralds of the Muse. Not in plenty, not in a thriving,
well-to-do condition, she delighteth. He that would sacrifice at her altar must not leave a few flowers, an apple, or some
symbolic gift. No; he must relinquish orchards and gardens,
prosperity and convenience; he may live on a heath without
trees; sometimes hungry, and sometimes rheumatic with cold.
The fire retreats and concentrates within into a pure flame, pure
as the stars to which it mounts.   1370

THE LORD'S SUPPER

(His Resignation as Minister Explained. Boston, 1832)

It was only too probable that among the half-converted Pagans, and Jews, any rite, any form, would find favor, whilst yet unable to comprehend the spiritual character of Christianity.   1371

It has seemed to me that the use of this ordinance tends to produce confusion in our views of the relation of the soul to God. It is the old objection to the doctrine of the Trinity,— that the true worship was transferred from God to Christ, or that such confusion was introduced into the soul that an undivided worship was given nowhere. Is not that the effect of the Lord's Supper? * * * For the service does not stand upon the basis of a voluntary act, but is imposed by authority.
                                                                1372

I am so much a Unitarian as this: that I believe the human mind can admit but one God, and that every effort to pay religious homage to more than one being goes to take away all right ideas.   1373

In the moment when you make the least petition to God, though it be but a silent wish that he may approve you, or add one moment to your life,—do you not, in the very act, necessarily exclude all other beings from your thought? In that act, the soul stands alone with God, and Jesus is no more present to your mind than your brother or your child. 1374

Most men find the bread and wine no aid to devotion, and to some it is a painful impediment. To eat bread is one thing; to love the precepts of Christ and resolve to obey them is quite another.   1375

I am not so foolish as to declaim against forms. Forms
are as essential as bodies; but to exalt particular forms, to
adhere to one form a moment after it is outgrown, is unreason-
able, and it is alien to the spirit of Christ.　　　　　1376

If I understand the distinction of Christianity, the reason
why it is to be preferred over all other systems and is divine
is this, that it is a moral system; that it presents men with
truths which are their own reason, and enjoins practices that
are their own justification; that if miracles may be said to have
been its evidence to the first Christians they are not its evidence to us, but the doctrines themselves; that every practice
is Christian which praises itself, and every practice unchristian
which condemns itself. I am not engaged to Christianity
by decent forms, or saving ordinances; it is not usage, it is
not what I do not understand, that binds me to it.　　　　1377

What I revere and obey in it (Christianity) is its reality,
its boundless charity, its deep interior life, the rest it gives to
mind, the echo it returns to my thoughts, the perfect accord
it makes with my reason through all its representation of God
and His Providence; and the persuasion and courage that come
out thence to lead me upward and onward. Freedom is the
essence of this faith. It has for its object simply to make
men good and wise. Its institutions then should be as flexible
as the wants of men. That form out of which the life and
suitableness have departed should be as worthless in its eyes
as the dead leaves that are falling around us.　　　　　1378

In the midst of considerations as to what Paul thought, and
why he so thought, I cannot help feeling that it is time mis-
spent to argue to or from his convictions, or those of Luke
and John, respecting any form. I seem to lose the substance
in seeking the shadow.　　　　　1379

That for which Paul lived and died so gloriously; that for which Jesus gave himself to be crucified; the end that animated the thousand martyrs and heroes who have followed his steps, was to redeem us from a formal religion, and teach us to seek our well-being in the formation of the soul.   1380

It is my desire, in the office of a Christian minister, to do nothing which I cannot do with my whole heart. Having said this, I have said all. I have no hostility to this institution; I am only stating my want of sympathy with it. Neither should I ever have obtruded this opinion upon other people, had I not been called by my office to administer it. That is the end of my opposition, that I am not interested in it. I am content that it stand to the end of the world, if it please men and please Heaven, and I shall rejoice in all the good it produces. As it is the prevailing opinion and feeling in our religious community that it is an indispensable part of the pastoral office to administer this ordinance, I am about to resign into your hands that office which you have confided to me.   1381

A LETTER

To Martin Van Buren, President

A Protest Against the Proposed Removal of the Cherokee Indians from the State of Georgia, 1838

In speaking thus the sentiments of my neighbors and my own, perhaps I overstep the bounds of decorum. But would it not be a higher indecorum coldly to argue a matter like this? We only state the fact that a crime is projected that confounds our understandings by its magnitude,—a crime that really deprives us as well as the Cherokees of a country? for how could we call the conspiracy that should crush these poor Indians our government, or the land that was cursed by their parting and dying imprecations our country, any more? You, sir, will bring down that renowned chair in which you sit into infamy if your seal is set to this instrument of perfidy; and the name of this nation, hitherto the sweet omen of religion and liberty, will stink to the world.   1382

One circumstance lessens the reluctance with which I intrude at this time on your attention my conviction that the government ought to be admonished of a new historical fact, which the discussion of this question has disclosed, namely, that there exists in a great part of the Northern people a gloomy diffidence in the *moral* character of the government.   1383

A man with your experience in affairs must have seen cause to appreciate the futility of opposition to the moral sentiment. However feeble the sufferer and however great the oppressor, it is in the nature of things that the blow should recoil upon the aggressor. For God is in the sentiment, and it cannot be withstood. The potentate and the people perish before it; but with it, and as its executor, they are omnipotent.   1384

ADDRESS

Emancipation of the Negroes in the
British West Indies—1844

I shall not apologize for my weakness.   In this cause, no
man's weakness is any prejudice; it has a thousand sons; if
one man cannot speak, ten others can; and, whether by the
wisdom of its friends, or by the folly of the adversaries; by
speech and by silence; by doing and by omitting to do, it goes
forward.   1385

The hardest selfishness is to be borne with. Let us withhold
every reproachful, and, if we can, every indignant remark.   In
this cause, 'we must renounce our temper, and the risings of
pride.   If there be any man who thinks the ruin of a race
of men a small matter, compared with the last decoration and
completions of his own comfort,—who would not so much as
part with his ice-cream, to save them from rapine and manacles,
I think I must not hesitate to satisfy that man that also his
cream and vanilla are safer and cheaper by placing the negro
nation on a fair footing than by robbing them.   1386

But the crude element of good in human affairs must work
and ripen, spite of whips and plantation laws and West Indian
interest.   Conscience rolled on its pillow, and could not sleep.
                                                            1387

I said, this event is signal in the history of civilization.
There are many styles of civilization, and not one only.   Ours
is full of barbarities.   1388

[249]

Virtuous men will not again rely on political agents. They have found out the deleterious effect of political association. Up to this day we have allowed to statesmen a paramount social standing, and we bow low to them as to the great. We cannot extend this deference to them any longer. The secret cannot be kept, that the seats of power are filled by underlings, ignorant, timid and selfish to a degree to destroy all claim, excepting that on compassion, to the society of the just and generous. What happened notoriously to an American ambassador in England, that he found himself compelled to palter and to disguise the fact that he was a slave-breeder, happens to men of state. Their vocation is a presumption against them among well-meaning people. The superstition respecting power and office is going to the ground. The stream of human affairs flows its own way, and is very little affected by the activity of legislators. What great masses of men wish done, will be done; and they do not wish it for a freak, but because it is their state and natural end.   1389

When at last in a race a new principle appears, an idea,— *that* conserves it; ideas only save races.   1390

All the songs and newspapers and money subscriptions and vituperation of such as do not think with us, will avail nothing against a fact. I say to you, you must save yourself, black or white, man or woman; other help is none. I esteem the occasion of this jubilee to be the proud discovery that the black race can contend with the white; that in the great anthem which we call history, a piece of many parts and vast compass, after playing a long time a very low and subdued accompaniment, they perceive the time arrived when they can strike in with effect and take a master's part in the music. The civility of the world has reached that pitch that their moral genius is becoming indispensable, and the quality of this race is to be honored for itself. For this, they have been preserved in sandy deserts, in rice-swamps, in kitchens and shoe-shops, so long; now let them emerge, clothed and in their own form.   1391

America is not civil, whilst Africa is barbarous.   1392

WAR

(1838)

It has been a favorite study of modern philosophy to indicate the steps of human progress, to watch the rising of a thought in one man's mind, the communication of it to a few, to a small minority, its expansion and general reception, until it publishes itself to the world by destroying the existing laws and institutions, and the generation of new.   1393

In the infancy of society, when a thin population and improvidence make the supply of food and of shelter insufficient and very precarious, and when hunger, thirst, ague and frozen limbs universally take precedence of the wants of the mind and the heart, the necessities of the strong will certainly be satisfied at the cost of the weak, at whatever peril of future revenge.   1394

It is the ignorant and childish part of mankind that is the fighting part.   Idle and vacant minds want excitement, as all boys kill cats. *** The boxer's ring is the enjoyment of the part of society whose animal nature alone has been developed.
1395

As all history is the picture of war, as we have said, so it is no less true that it is the record of the mitigation and decline of war.   1396

[251]

The popes, to their eternal honor, declared religious jubilees, during which all hostilities were suspended throughout Christendom, and man had a breathing space.   1397

All history is the decline of war, though the slow decline. All that society has yet gained is mitigation; the doctrine of the right of war still remains.   1398

It is not a great matter how long men refuse to believe the advent of peace; war is on its last legs; and a universal peace is as sure as is the prevalence of civilization over barbarism, of liberal government over feudal forms.   The question for us is only *How soon?*   1399

What is the best must be the true; and what is true—that is, what is at bottom fit and agreeable to the constitution of man—must at last prevail over all obstruction and all opposition.   1400

There is no good now enjoyed by society that was not once as problematical and visionary as this (universal peace).   1401

You shall hear, some day, of a wild fancy which some man has in his brain, of the mischief of secret oaths.   Come again one or two years afterwards, and you shall see it has built great houses of solid wood and brick and mortar.   You shall see a hundred presses printing a million sheets; you shall see men and horses and wheels made to walk, run and roll for it; this great body of matter thus executing that one man's wild thought.   1402

War and peace thus resolve themselves into a mercury of the state of cultivation. At a certain stage of his progress, the man fights, if he be of a sound body and mind. At a certain higher stage, he makes no offensive demonstration, but is alert to repel injury, and of an unconquerable heart. At a still higher stage, he comes into the region of holiness; passion has passed away from him; his warlike nature is all converted into an active medicinal principle; he sacrifices himself, and accepts with alacrity wearisome tasks of denial and charity; but, being attacked, he bears it and turns the other cheek, as one engaged, throughout his being, no longer to the service of an individual, but to the common soul of all men.   1403

A man does not come the length of the spirit of martyrdom without some active purpose, some equal motive, some flaming love.   1404

If you have a nation of men who have risen to that height of moral cultivation that they will not declare war or carry arms, for they have not so much madness left in their brains, you have a nation of lovers, of benefactors, of true, great and able men. Let me know more of that nation; I shall not find them defenceless, with idle hands swinging at their sides. I shall find them men of love, honor and truth; men of an immense industry; men whose influence is felt to the end of the earth; men whose very look and voice carry the sentence of honor and shame; and all forces yield to their energy and persuasion.   1405

Everything great must be done in the spirit of greatness.
1406

The cause of peace is not the cause of cowardice. If peace is sought to be defended or preserved for the safety of the luxurious and the timid, it is a sham, and the peace will be base.   1407

THE FUGITIVE SLAVE LAW

Concord Speech, 1851

The last year has forced us all into politics, and made it a paramount duty to seek what it is often a duty to shun. We do not breathe well. There is infamy in the air. I have a new experience. I wake in the morning with a painful sensation, which I carry about all day, and which, when traced home, is the odious remembrance of that ignominy which has fallen on Massachusetts, which robs the landscape of beauty, and takes the sunshine out of every hour.   1408

One intellectual benefit we owe to the late disgraces. The crisis had the illuminating power of a sheet of lightning at midnight. It showed truth. It ended a good deal of nonsense we had been wont to hear and to repeat, on the 19th of April, the 17th of June, the 4th of July. It showed the slightness and unreliableness of our social fabric, it showed what stuff reputations are made of, what straws we dignify by office and title, and how competent we are to give counsel and help in a day of trial. It showed the shallowness of leaders; the divergence of parties from their alleged grounds; showed that men would not stick to what they had said, that the resolutions of public bodies, or the pledges never so often given and put on record of public men will not bind them. The fact comes out more plainly that you cannot rely on any man for the defence of truth, who is not constitutionally or by blood and temperament on that side. A man of a greedy and unscrupulous selfishness may maintain morals when they are in fashion; but he will not stick.   1409

The popular assumption that all men loved freedom, and believed in the Christian religion, was found hollow American brag; only persons who were known and tried benefactors are found standing for freedom; the sentimentalists went downstream. I question the value of our civilization, when I see that the public mind had never less hold of the strongest of all truths. The sense of injustice is blunted,—a sure sign of the shallowness of our intellect.   1410

Nothing proves the 'want of all thought, the absence of standard in men's minds,—more than the dominion of party.

1411

The crisis is interesting as it shows the self-protecting nature of the world and of the Divine laws. It is the law of the world,—as much immorality as there is, so much misery. The greatest prosperity will in vain resist the greatest calamity.

1412

Here is a statute which enacts the crime of kidnapping,—a crime on one footing with arson and murder. A man's right to liberty is as inalienable as his right to life.   1413

If our resistance to this law is not right, there is no right. This is not meddling with other people's affairs; this is hindering other people from meddling with us.   1414

Laws are merely declaratory of the natural sentiments of mankind, and the language of all permanent laws will be in contradiction to any immoral enactment. And thus it happens here: Statute fights against Statute. By the law of Congress, March 2, 1807, it is piracy and murder, punishable with death, to enslave a man on the coast of Africa. By law of Congress, September, 1850, it is a high crime and misdemeanor, punishable with fine and imprisonment, to resist the re-enslaving a man on the coast of America. Off soundings, it is piracy and murder to enslave him. On soundings, it is fine and prison not to re-enslave. What kind of legislation is this? What kind of constitution which covers it?   1415

A wicked law cannot be executed by good men, and must
be by bad. Flagitious men must be employed, and every act
of theirs is a stab at the public peace. It cannot be executed
at such a cost, and so it brings a bribe in its hand. This law
comes with infamy in it, and out of it. It offers a bribe in
its own clauses for the consummation of the crime. To serve
it, low and mean people are found by the groping of the
government. No government ever found it hard to pick up
tools for base actions.   1416

Great is the mischief of a legal crime. Every person who
touches this business is contaminated. There has not been in
our lifetime another moment when public men were personally
lowered by their political action.   1417

We poor men in the country who might once have thought
it an honor to shake hands with them, or to dine at their
boards, would now shrink from their touch, nor could they
enter our humblest doors. You have a law which no man
can obey, or abet the obeying, without loss of self-respect and
forfeiture of the name of gentleman.   1418

We shall one day bring the States shoulder to shoulder and
the citizens man to man to exterminate slavery. Why in the
name of common sense and the peace of mankind is not this
made the subject of instant negotiation and settlement?   1419

Nothing is impracticable to this nation, which it shall set
itself to do.   1420

Let us respect the Union to all honest ends.   But also respect an older and wider union, the law of Nature and rectitude. Massachusetts is as strong as the Universe, when it does that.

1421

Every nation and every man bows, in spite of himself, to a higher mental and moral existence; and the sting of the late disgraces is that this royal position of Massachusetts was foully lost, that the well-known sentiment of her people was not expressed.   Let us correct this error.   In this one fastness let truth be spoken and right done.   1422

THE FUGITIVE SLAVE LAW

1854

The one thing not to be forgiven to intellectual persons is, not to know their own task, or to take their ideas from others. From this want of manly rest in their own and rash acceptance of other people's watchwords come the imbecility and fatigue of their conversation. For they cannot affirm these from any original experience, and of course not with the natural movement and total strength of their nature and talent, but only from their memory, only from their cramped position of standing for their teacher.   1423

The way in which the country was dragged to consent to this, and the disastrous defection (on the miserable cry of Union) of the men of letters, of the colleges, of educated men, nay, of some preachers of religion,—was the darkest passage in the history. It showed that our prosperity had hurt us, and that we could not be shocked by crime. It showed that the old religion and the sense of right had faded and gone out; that while we reckoned ourselves a highly cultivated nation, our bellies had run away with our brains, and the principles of culture and progress did not exist.   1424

We never get beyond our first lesson, for, really, the world exists, as I understand it, to teach the science of liberty, which begins with liberty from fear.   1425

One would have said that a Christian would not keep slaves; —but the Christians keep slaves. Of course they will not dare to read the Bible? Won't they? They quote the Bible, quote Paul, quote Christ, to justify slavery. If slavery is good, then is lying, theft, arson, homicide, each and all good.   1426

Covenants are of no use without honest men to keep them; laws of none but with loyal citizens to obey them. To interpret Christ it needs Christ in the heart. The teachings of the Spirit can be apprehended only by the same spirit that gave them forth. To make good the cause of Freedom, you must draw off from all foolish trust in others. You must be citadels and warriors yourselves, declarations of Independence, the charter, the battle and the victory.   1427

We have many teachers; we are in this world for culture, to be instructed in realities, in the laws of moral and intelligent nature; and our education is not conducted by toys and luxuries, but by austere and rugged masters, by poverty, solitude, passions, War, Slavery; to know that Paradise is under the shadow of swords; that divine sentiments which are always soliciting us are breathed into us from on high, and are an offset to a Universe of suffering and crime; that self-reliance, the height and perfection of man, is reliance on God.   1428

Whenever a man has come to this mind, that there is no Church for him but his believing prayer; no Constitution but his dealing well and justly with his neighbor; no liberty but his invincible will to do right,—then certain aids and allies will promptly appear; for the constitution of the Universe is on his side. It is of no use to vote down gravitation of morals.
                   1429

What is useful will last, whilst that which is hurtful to the world will sink beneath all the opposing forces which it must exasperate.   1430

The end for which man was made is not crime in any form, and a man cannot steal without incurring the penalties of the thief, though all the legislatures vote that it is virtuous, and though there be a general conspiracy among scholars and official persons to hold him up, and to say, "Nothing is good but stealing." A man who commits a crime defeats the end of his existence. 1431

A man who steals another man's labor steals away his own faculties; his integrity, his humanity is flowing away from him. The habit of oppression cuts out the moral eyes, and, though the intellect goes on simulating the moral as before, its sanity is gradually destroyed. *** American slavery affords no exception to this rule. 1432

The plea in the mouth of the slave-holder that the negro is an inferior race sounds very oddly in my ear. "The masters of slaves seem generally anxious to prove that they are not of a race superior in any noble quality to the meanest of their bondmen." 1433

Liberty is never cheap. It is made difficult, because freedom is the accomplishment and perfectness of man. He is a finished man; earning and bestowing good; equal to the world; at home in Nature and dignifying that; the sun does not see anything nobler, and has nothing to teach him. Therefore mountains of difficulty must be surmounted, stern trials met, wiles of seduction, dangers, healed by a quarantine of calamities, to measure his strength before he dare say, I am free. 1434

Let the aid of virtue, intelligence and education be cast where they rightfully belong. They are organically ours. Let them be loyal to their own. I wish to see the instructed class here know their own flag, and not fire on their comrades. We should not forgive the clergy for taking on every issue the immoral side; nor the Bench, if it put itself on the side of the culprit; nor the Government, if it sustain the mob against the laws. 1435

It is a potent support and ally to a brave man standing single, or with a few, for the right, and out-voted and ostracized, to know that better men in other parts of the country appreciate the service and will rightly report him to his own and the next age.   1436

But I put it to every noble and generous spirit, to every poetic, every heroic, every religious heart, that not so is our learning, our education, our poetry, our worship to be declared. Liberty is aggressive.   Liberty is the Crusade of all brave and conscientious men, the Epic Poetry, the new religion, the chivalry of all gentlemen.   This is the oppressed Lady whom true knights on their oath and honor must rescue and save.
                                                      1437

JOHN BROWN

Boston Speech—1859

He is a man to make friends wherever on earth courage and integrity are esteemed, the rarest of heroes, a pure idealist, with no by-ends of his own.   1438

It is easy to see what a favorite he will be with history, which plays such pranks with temporary reputations. Nothing can resist the sympathy which all elevated minds must feel with Brown, and through them the whole civilized world; and if he must suffer, he must drag official gentlemen into an immortality most undesirable, of which they have already some disagreeable forebodings.   1439

I said John Brown was an idealist. He believed in his ideas to that extent that he existed to put them all into action; he said he did not believe in moral suasion, he believed in putting the thing through. He saw how deceptive the forms are.   1440

If judges cannot find law enough to maintain the sovereignty of the state, and to protect the life and freedom of every inhabitant not a criminal, it is idle to compliment them as learned and venerable.   1441

JOHN BROWN

Salem Speech—1860

(When but a boy), it chanced that in Pennsylvania, where he was sent by his father to collect cattle, he fell in with a boy whom he heartily liked and whom he looked upon as his superior. This boy was a slave; he saw him beaten with an iron shovel, and otherwise maltreated; he saw that this boy had nothing better to look forward to in life, whilst he himself was petted and made much of; for he was much considered in the family where he then stayed, from the circumstance that this boy of twelve years had conducted alone a drove of cattle a hundred miles. But the colored boy had no friend, and no future. This worked such indignation in him that he swore an oath of resistance to slavery as long as he lived. And thus his enterprise to go into Virginia and run off five hundred or a thousand slaves was not a piece of spite or revenge, a plot of two years or of twenty years, but the keeping of an oath made to heaven and earth forty-seven years before.   1442

It is impossible to see courage, and disinterestedness, and the love that casts out fear, without sympathy. All women are drawn to him by their predominance of sentiment. All gentlemen, of course, are on his side. I do not mean by "gentlemen", people of scented hair and perfumed handkerchiefs, but men of gentle blood and generosity.   1443

AMERICAN CIVILIZATION

Speech Urging Emancipation—1862

Use, labor of each for all, is the health and virtue of all beings. *Ich dien,* I serve, is a truly royal motto. And it is the mark of nobleness to volunteer the lowest service, the greatest spirit only attaining to humility. Nay, God is God because he is the servant of all. 1444

Labor; a man coins himself into his labor; turns his day, his strength, his thought, his affection into some product which remains as the visible sign of his power; and to protect that, to secure that to him, to secure his past self to his future self, is the object of all government. There is no interest in any country so imperative as that of labor; it covers all, and constitutions and governments exist for that,—to protect and insure it to the laborer. 1445

We have attempted to hold together two states of civilization; a higher state, where labor and the tenure of land and the right of suffrage are democratical; and a lower state, in which the old military tenure of prisoners or slaves, and of power and land in a few hands, makes an oligarchy; we have attempted to hold these two states of society under one law. But the rude and early state of society does not work well with the later, nay, works badly, and has poisoned politics, public morals and social intercourse. 1446

We live in a new and exceptionable age. America is another word for Opportunity. Our whole history appears like a last effort of the Divine Providence in behalf of the human race. 1447

In this national crisis, it is not argument that we want, but that rare courage which dares commit itself to a principle.
1448

Government must not be a parish clerk, a justice of the peace. It has, of necessity, in any crisis of the state, the absolute powers of a dictator.   1449

There are Scriptures written invisibly on men's hearts, whose letters do not come out until they are enraged. They can be read by war-fires, and by eyes in the last peril.   1450

Here again is a new occasion (the proposed emancipation of slaves) which heaven offers to sense and virtue. It looks as if we held the fate of the fairest possession of mankind in our hands, to be saved by our firmness or to be lost by hesitation.   1451

It is very certain that the statesman who shall break through the cobwebs of doubt, fear and petty cavil that lie in the way, will be greeted by the unanimous thanks of mankind.   1452

THE EMANCIPATION PROCLAMATION

Speech at Boston—September, 1862

In so many arid forms which states encrust themselves with, once in a century, if so often, a poetic act and record occur. These are the jets of thought into affairs, when, roused by danger or inspired by genius, the political leaders of the day break the else insurmountable routine of class and local legislation, and take a step forward in the direction of catholic and universal interests. Every step in the history of political liberty is a sally of the human mind into the untried Future, and has the interest of genius, and is fruitful in heroic anecdotes. Liberty is a slow fruit. It comes, like religion, for short periods, and in rare conditions, as if awaiting a culture of the race which shall make it organic and permanent. 1453

He (Lincoln) has been permitted to do more for America than any other American man. He is well entitled to the most indulgent construction. Forget all that we thought shortcomings, every mistake, every delay. In the extreme embarrassments of his part, call these endurance, wisdom, magnanimity; illuminated, as they now are, by this dazzling success. 1454

Against all timorous counsels he (Lincoln) had the courage to seize the moment; and such was his position, and such the felicity attending the action, that he has replaced government in the good graces of mankind. 1455

The government has assured itself of the best constituency in the world; every spark of intellect, every virtuous feeling, every religious heart, every man of honor, every poet, every philosopher, the generosity of the cities, the health of the country, the strong arms of the mechanic, the endurance of farmers, the passionate conscience of women, the sympathy of distant nations,—all rally to its support. 1456

Every acre in the free states gained substantial value on the twenty-second of September.   The cause of disunion and war has been reached and begun to be removed.   1457

The war existed long before the cannonade of Sumter, and could not be postponed.   It might have begun otherwise or elsewhere, but war was in the minds and bones of the combatants, it was written on the iron leaf, and you might as easily dodge gravitation.   1458

We think we cannot overstate the wisdom and benefit of this act of the government.   1459

Meantime that ill-fated, much-injured race which the Proclamation respects will lose somewhat of the dejection sculptured for ages in their bronzed countenance, uttered in the wailing of their plaintive music,—a race naturally benevolent, docile, industrious, and whose very miseries sprang from their great talent for usefulness, which, in a moral age, will not only defend their independence, but will give them a rank among nations.   1460

WOMAN

1855

Man is the will, and Woman the sentiment. In this ship of humanity, Will is the rudder, and Sentiment, the sail; when Woman affects to steer, the rudder is only a masked sail.   1461

But there is an art which is better than painting, poetry, music, or architecture,—better than botany, geology, or any science;—namely, Conversation. Wise, cultivated, genial conversation is the last flower of civilization and the best result which life has to offer us,—a cup for gods, which has no repentance. Conversation is our account of ourselves. All we have, all we can, all we know, is brought into play, and as the reproduction, in finer form, of all our havings.

Women are, by this and their social influence, the civilizers of mankind.   1462

They finish society, manners, language. Form and ceremony are their realm. They embellish trifles. All these ceremonies that hedge our life around are not to be despised, and when we have become habituated to them, cannot be dispensed with. No woman can despise them with impunity. Their genius delights in ceremonies, in forms, in decorating life with manners, with properties, order and grace.   1463

There is no grace that is taught by the dancing-master, no style adopted into the etiquette of courts, but was first the whim and the mere action of some brilliant woman, who charmed beholders by this new expression, and made it remembered and copied.   1464

More vulnerable, more infirm, more mortal than men, they could not be such excellent artists in this element of fancy if they did not lend and give themselves to it. They are poets who believe their own poetry.   1465

There is much in their nature, much in their social position which gives them a certain power of divination. And women know, at first sight, the characters of those with whom they converse. There is much that tends to give them a religious height which men do not attain. Their sequestration from affairs and from the injury to the moral sense which affairs often inflict, aids this. And in every remarkable religious development in the world, women have taken a leading part.   1466

The aspiration of this century will be the code of the next.
1467

Let us have the true woman, the adorner, the hospitable, the religious heart, and no lawyer need be called in to write stipulations, the cunning clauses of provision, the strong investitures;—for woman moulds the lawgiver and writes the law.
1468

Slavery it is that makes slavery; freedom, freedom. The slavery of women happened when the men were slaves of kings.
1469

THE FORTUNE OF THE REPUBLIC

Our sleepy civilization, ever since Roger Bacon and Monk Schwartz invented gunpowder, has built its whole art of war, all fortification by land and sea, all drill and military education, on that one compound,—all is an extension of a gun-barrel.

1470

When the cannon is aimed by ideas, when men with religious convictions are behind it, when men die for what they live for, and the mainspring that works daily urges them to hazard all, then the cannon articulates its explosions with the voice of a man, then the rifle seconds the cannon and the fowling-piece the rifle, and the women make the cartridges, and all shoot at one mark; then gods join in the combat; then poets are born, and the better code of laws at last records the victory.

1471

If a temperate wise man should look over our American society, I think the first danger that would excite his alarm would be the European influences on this country.

1472

A man does not want to be sun-dazzled, sun-blind; but every man must have glimmer enough to keep him from knocking his head against the walls.

1473

Let us realize that this country, the last found, is the great charity of God to the human race.

1474

The end of all political struggle is to establish morality as the basis of all legislation.

1475

MICHAEL ANGELO

Whilst his name belongs to the highest class of genius, his life contains in it no injurious influence. Every line in his biography might be read to the human race with wholesome effect. The means, the materials of his activity, were coarse enough to be appreciated, being addressed for the most part to the eye; the results, sublime and all innocent. A purity severe and even terrible goes out from the lofty productions of his pencil and his chisel, and again from the more perfect sculpture of his own life, which heals and exalts.   1476

Above all men whose history we know, Michael Angelo presents us with the perfect image of the artist. He is an eminent master in the four fine arts, Painting, Sculpture, Architecture and Poetry. In three of them by visible means, and in poetry by words, he strove to express the Idea of Beauty. This idea possessed him and determined all his activity. Beauty in the largest sense, beauty inward and outward, comprehending grandeur as a part, and reaching to goodness as its soul,—this to receive and this to impart, was his genius.   1477

It is a happiness to find, amid the falsehood and griefs of the human race, a soul at intervals born to behold and create only Beauty. So shall not the indescribable charm of the natural world, the great spectacle of morn and evening which shut and open the most disastrous day, want observers.   1478

The common eye is satisfied with the surface on which it rests. The wise eye knows that it is surface, and, if beautiful, only the result of interior harmonies, which, to him who knows them, compose the image of higher beauty.   1479

Man is the highest, and indeed the only proper object of
plastic art.   1480

There is a closer relation than is commonly thought between
the fine arts and the useful arts; and it is an essential fact in
the history of Michael Angelo that his love of beauty is made
solid and perfect by his deep understanding of the mechanic
arts.   Architecture is the bond that unites the elegant and the
economical arts, and his skill in this is a pledge of his capacity
in both kinds.   1481

And not only was this discoverer of Beauty, and its teacher
among men, rooted and grounded in those severe laws of practical skill, which genius can never teach, and which must be
learned by practice alone, but he was one of the most industrious
men that ever lived.   1482

Such was his devotion to art.   But let no man suppose that
the images which his spirit 'worshipped were mere transcripts
of external grace, or that this profound soul was taken or
holden in the chains of superficial beauty.   To him, of all men,
it was transparent.   Through it he beheld the eternal spiritual
beauty which ever clothes itself with grand and graceful out-
lines, as its appropriate form.   He called external grace "the
frail and weary weed, in which God dresses the soul which he
has called into Time."   1483

He sought, through the eye, to reach the soul.   Therefore,
as, in the first place, he sought to approach the Beautiful by
the study of the True, so he failed not to make the next step
of progress, and to seek Beauty in its highest form, that of
Goodness.   The sublimity of his art is in his life.   1484

He shared Dante's "deep contempt of the vulgar, not of the simple inhabitants of lowly streets or humble cottages, but of that sordid and abject crowd of all classes and all places who obscure, as much as in them lies, every beam of beauty in the universe." In like manner, he possessed an intense love of solitude. He lived alone, and never or very rarely took his meals with any person. 1485

Michael Angelo was of that class of men who are too superior to the multitude around them to command a full and perfect sympathy. 1486

It has been the defect of some great men that they did not duly appreciate or did not confess the talents and virtues of others, and so lacked one of the richest sources of happiness, and one of the best elements of humanity. 1487

There is yet one more trait in Michael Angelo's history, which humanizes his character without lessening its loftiness; this is his platonic love. He was deeply enamoured of the most accomplished lady of the time, Vittoria Colonna, the widow of the Marquis di Pescara, who, after the death of her husband, devoted herself to letters, and to the writing of religious poetry. She was also an admirer of his genius, and came to Rome repeatedly to see him. To her his sonnets are addressed; and they all breathe a chaste and divine regard, unparalleled in any amatory poetry except that of Dante and Petrarch. They are founded on the thought that beauty is the virtue of the body, as virtue is the beauty of the soul; that a beautiful person is sent into the world as an image of the divine beauty, not to provoke but to purify the sensual into intellectual and divine love. He enthrones his mistress as a benignant angel, who is to refine and perfect his own character. 1488

He was not a citizen of any country; he belonged to the human race; he was a brother and a friend to all who acknowledge the beauty that beams in universal Nature, and who seek by labor and self-denial to approach its source in perfect goodness. 1489

POWERS AND LAWS OF THOUGHT

I believe in the existence of the material world as the expression of the spiritual or the real, and in the impenetrable mystery which hides (and hides through absolute transparency) the mental nature, I await the insight which our advancing knowledge of material laws shall furnish.   1490

Whilst we converse with truths as thoughts, they exist also as plastic forces; as the soul of a man, the soul of a plant, the genius or constitution of any part of Nature, which makes it what it is.   1491

My belief in the use of a course on philosophy is that the student shall learn to appreciate the miracle of the mind; shall learn its subtle but immense power, or shall begin to learn it; shall come to know that in seeing and in no tradition he must find what truth is; that he shall see in it the source of all traditions, and shall see each one of them as better or worse statement of its revelations; shall come to trust it entirely, as the only true; to cleave to God against the name of God.   1492

Yes, 'tis a great vice in all countries, the sacrifice of scholars to be courtiers and diners-out, to talk for the amusement of those who wish to be amused, though the stars of heaven must be plucked down and packed into rockets to this end. What with egotism on one side and levity on the other, we shall have no Olympus.   1493

What is life but the angle of vision? A man is measured
by the angle at which he looks at objects. What is life but
what a man is thinking of all day? This is his fate and his
employer. Knowing is the measure of the man. By how
much we know, so much we are.   1494

I think metaphysics a grammar to which, once read, we
seldom return.   1495

I think that philosophy is still rude and elementary. It
will one day be taught by poets. The poet is in the natural
attitude; he is believing; the philosopher, after some struggle,
having only reasons for believing.   1496

To Be is the unsolved, unsolvable wonder. To Be, in its
two connections of inward and outward, the mind and Nature.
The wonder subsists, and age, though of eternity, could not
approach a solution.   1497

I am of the oldest religion. Leaving aside the question which
was prior, egg or bird, I believe the mind is the creator of the
world, and is ever creating;—that at last Matter is dead Mind;
that mind makes the senses it sees with; that the genius of man
is a continuation of the power that made him and that has
not done making him.   1498

I dare not deal with this element in its pure essence. It
is too rare for the wings of words. Yet I see that Intellect
is a science of degrees, and that as man is conscious of the law
of vegetable and animal nature, so he is aware of an Intellect,
which overhangs his consciousness like a sky, of degree above
degree, of heaven within heaven.   1499

Our eating, trading, marrying and learning are mistaken by us for ends and realities, whilst they are properly symbols only; when we have come, by a divine leading, into the inner firmament, we are apprised of the unreality or representative character of what we esteemed final. 1500

There are those who disputing will make you dispute, and the nervous and hysterical and animalized will produce a like series of symptoms in you, though no other persons ever evoke the like phenomena, and though you are conscious that they do not properly belong to you, but are a sort of extension of the diseases of this particular person into you. 1501

In unfit company the finest powers are paralyzed. No ambition, no oppositon, no friendly attention and fostering kindness, no wine, music or exhilarating aids, neither warm fireside nor fresh air, walking or riding, avail at all to resist the palsy of mis-association. Genius is mute, is dull; there is no genius. Ask of your flowers to open when you have let in on them a freezing wind. 1502

Let me whisper a secret; nobody ever forgives any admiration in you of them, any overestimate of what they do or have.
1503

There is always a loss of truth and power when a man leaves working for himself to work for another. Absolutely speaking, I can only work for myself. All my good is magnetic, and I educate not by lessons but by going about my business. When, moved by love, a man teaches his child or joins with his neighbor in any act of common benefit, or spends himself for his friend, or rushes at immense personal sacrifice on some public, self-immolating act, it is not done for others, but to fulfil a high necessity of his proper character. 1504

The air rings with sounds, but only a few vibrations can reach our tympanum.   Perhaps creatures live with us which we never see, because their motion is too swift for our vision. The sun may shine, or a galaxy of suns; you will get no more light than your eye will hold.   (Written 50 years before Radio.)   1505

The healthy mind lies parallel to the currents of Nature and sees things in place, or makes discoveries.   1506

Instinct is our name for the potential wit.   1507

For thought exists to be expressed.   That which cannot externize itself is not thought.   1508

Do not trifle with your perceptions, or hold them cheap. They are your door to the seven heavens, and if you pass it by you will miss your way.   1509

The conduct of Intellect must respect nothing so much as preserving the sensibility.   My measure for all subjects of science as of events is their impression on the soul.   That mind is best which is most impressionable.   There are times when the cawing of a crow, a weed, a snow-flake, a boy's willow whistle, or a farmer planting in his field is more suggestive to the mind than the Yosemite gorge or the Vatican would be in another hour.   In like mood an old verse, or certain words, gleam with rare significance.   1510

Goethe, the surpassing intellect of modern times, apprehends the spiritual but is not spiritual.   1511

Talent is habitual facility of execution.   We like people who can do things.   1512

The secret of power, intellectual or physical, is concentration, and all concentration involves of necessity a certain narrowness.   1513

It is much to write sentences; it is more to add method and write out the spirit of your life symmetrically.   1514

The world stands by balanced antagonisms.   The more the peculiarities are pressed, the better the result.   1515

We disown our debt to moral evil.   To science there is no poison; to botany no weed; to chemistry no dirt.   The curses of malignity and despair are important criticism, which must be heeded until he can explain and rightly silence them.   1516

There are two theories of life; one for the demonstration of our talent, the other for the education of the man.   One is activity, the busy-body, the following of that practical talent which we have, in the belief that what is so natural, easy and pleasant to us and desirable to others will surely lead us out safely; in this direction lie usefulness, comfort, society, low power of all sorts.   The other is trust, religion, consent to be nothing for eternity, entranced waiting, the worship of ideas. This is solitary, grand, secular.   They are in perpetual balance and strife.   One is talent, the other genius.   One is skill, the other character.   1517

A fact is only a fulcrum of the spirit. It is the terminus
of a past thought, but only a means now to new sallies of
the imagination and new progress of wisdom.   1518

Inspiration is the continuation of the divine effort that built
the man.   1519

Man was made for conflict, not for rest. In action is his
power; not in his goals but in his transitions man is great.
Instantly he is dwarfed by self-indulgence. The truest state
of mind rested in becomes false.   1520

Knowledge is plainly to be preferred before power, as being
that which guides and directs its blind force and impetus; but
Aristotle declares that the origin of reason is not reason, but
something better.   1521

Profound sincerity is the only basis of talent as of character.
        1522

INSTINCT AND INSPIRATION

Consciousness is but a taper in the great night; but the taper at which all the illumination of human arts and sciences was kindled.   1523

The eye and ear have a logic which transcends the skill of the tongue.   1524

The whole art of man has been an art of excitation, to provoke, to extort speech from the drowsy genius.   1525

The mark of the spirit is to know its way, to invent means.
                                                                1526

The only comfort I can lay to my own sorrow is that we have a higher than a personal interest, which, in the ruin of the personal, is secured. I see that all beauty of discourse or of manners lies in launching on the thought, and forgetting ourselves; and though the beatitude of the Intellect seems to lie out of our volition, and to be unattainable as the sky, yet we can take sight beforehand of a state of being wherein the will shall penetrate and control what it cannot now reach.
                                                                1527

Whence came all these tools, inventions, books, laws, parties, kingdoms? Out of the invisible world, through a few brains. Nineteen twentieths of their substance do trees draw from the air. Plant the pitch-pine in a sand-bank, where is no food, and it thrives, and presently makes a grove, and covers the sand with a soil by shedding its leaves.   1528

The secret of power is delight in one's work.   1529

There is a probity of the Intellect, which demands, if possible, virtues more costly than any Bible has consecrated. It consists in an absolute devotion to truth, founded in a faith in truth.   1530

Our books are full of generous biographies of Saints, who knew not that they were such.   1531

FROM THE DIAL

MODERN LITERATURE
1840

Let us not forget the genial miraculous force we have known to proceed from a book.   1532

In all ages, and now more, the narrow-minded have no interest in anything but in its relation to their personality.   1533

The great man, even whilst he relates a private fact personal to him, is really leading us away from him to an universal experience.   1534

PRAYERS
1842

If we can overhear the prayer we shall know the man.   1535

Let us not have the prayers of one sect, nor of the Christian Church, but of men in all ages and religions who have prayed well.   1536

EUROPE AND EUROPEAN BOOKS
1843

The poet, like the electric rod, must reach from a point nearer the sky than all surrounding objects, down to the earth, and into the dark wet soil, or neither is of use. The poet must not only converse with pure thought, but he must demonstrate it almost to the senses. His words must be pictures, his verses must be spheres and cubes, to be seen and smelled and handled.   1537

PAST AND PRESENT
1843

Truth is very old, but the merit of seers is not to invent but to dispose objects in their right places, and he is the commander who is always in the mount, whose eye not only sees details, but throws crowds of details into their right arrangement and a larger and juster totality than any other.

1538

Let no man think himself absolved because he does a generous action and befriends the poor, but let him see whether he so holds his property that a benefit goes from it to all.   1539

Time stills the loud noise of opinions, sinks the small, raises the great, so that the true emerges without effort and in perfect harmony to all eyes; but the truth of the present hour, except in particulars and single relations, is unattainable.   1540

The most elaborate history of to-day will have the oddest dislocated look in the next generation.   The historian of to-day is yet three ages off.   1541

The poet cannot descend into the turbid present without injury to his rarest gifts.   Hence that necessity of isolation which genius has always felt.   1542

But when the political aspects are so calamitous that the sympathies of the man overpower the habits of the poet, a higher than literary inspiration may succor him.   1543

The ancients are only venerable to us because distance has destroyed what was trivial.   1544

A LETTER

1843

One thing is plain, that discontent and the luxury of tears will bring nothing to pass.   1545

The pruning in the wild gardens of Nature is never forborne. Many of the best must die of consumption, many of despair, and many be stupid and insane, before the one great and fortunate life which they each predicted can shoot up into a thrifty and beneficent existence.   1546

THE TRAGIC

1844

He has seen but half the universe who never has been shown the house of Pain. As the salt sea covers more than two thirds of the surface of the globe, so sorrow encroaches in man on felicity. The conversation of men is a mixture of regrets and apprehensions.   1547

The bitterest tragic element in life to be derived from an intellectual source is the belief in a brute Fate or Destiny; the belief that the order of Nature and events is controlled by a law not adapted to man, nor man to that, but which holds on its way to the end, serving him if his wishes chance to lie in the same course, crushing him if his wishes lie contrary to it, and heedless whether it serves or crushes him.   1548

There are people who have an appetite for grief, pleasure is not strong enough and they crave pain, mithridatic stomachs which must be fed on poisoned bread, natures so doomed that no prosperity can soothe their ragged and dishevelled desolation. They mis-hear and mis-behold, they suspect and dread. They handle every nettle and ivy in the hedge, and tread on every snake in the meadow.   1549

Frankly, then, it is necessary to say that all sorrow dwells in a low region. It is superficial; for the most part fantastic, or in the appearance and not in things. Tragedy is in the eye of the observer, and not in the heart of the sufferer.   1550

Some men are above grief, and some below it. Few are capable of love. In phlegmatic natures calamity is unaffecting, in shallow natures it is rhetorical.   1551

All that life demands of us through the greater part of the day is an equilibrium, a readiness, open eyes and ears, and free hands. Society asks this, and truth, and love, and the genius of our life.   1552

We must walk as guests in Nature; not impassioned, but cool and disengaged. A man should try Time, and his face should wear the expression of a just judge, who has nowise made up his opinion, who fears nothing, and even hopes nothing, but who puts Nature and fortune on their merits; he will hear the case out, and then decide.   1553

Whilst a man is not grounded in the divine life by his proper roots, he clings by some tendrils of affection to society— mayhap to what is best and greatest in it, and in calm times it will not appear that he is adrift and not moored; but let any shock take place in society, any revolution of custom, of law, of opinion, and at once his type of permanence is shaken. The disorder of his neighbors appears to him universal disorder; chaos is come again.   But in truth he was already a driving wreck before the wind arose, which only revealed to him his vagabond state.   1554

Time the consoler, Time the rich carrier of all changes, dries the freshest tears by obtruding new figures, new costumes, new roads, on our eye, new voices on our ear.   1555

The intellect is a consoler, which delights in detaching or putting an interval between a man and his fortune, and so converts the sufferer into a spectator and his pain into poetry. It yields the joys of conversation, of letters and of science. Hence also the torments of life become tuneful tragedy, solemn and soft with music, and garnished with rich dark pictures. But higher still than the activities of art, the intellect in its purity and the moral sense in its purity are not distinguished from each other, and both ravish us into a region whereunto these passionate clouds of sorrow cannot rise.   1556

MISCELLANEOUS

The misery of man appears like childish petulance, when we explore the steady and prodigal provision that has been made for his support and delight on this green ball which floats him through the heavens.   1557
—*Commodity.*

It is not in distinguished circles that wisdom and elevated characters are usually found, or, if found, they are not confined thereto; and my recollections of the best hours go back to private conversations in different parts of the kingdom, with persons little known.   1558
—*English Traits, Personal.*

An Englishman shows no mercy to those below him in the social scale, as he looks for none from those above him; any forbearance from his superiors surprises him, and they suffer in his good opinion.   1559
—*English Traits, Result.*

It (England) is the land of patriots, martyrs, sages and bards, and if the ocean out of which it emerged should wash it away, it will be remembered as an island famous for immortal laws, for the announcement of original right which make the stone tables of liberty.   1560
—*English Traits, Result.*

If there be one test of national genius universally accepted, it is success; and if there be one successful country in the universe for the last millennium, that country is England.   1561
—*English Traits, Land.*

The American is only the continuation of the English genius into new conditions, more or less propitious.   1562
—*English Traits, Land.*

A scholar defending the cause of slavery, of arbitrary government, of monopoly, of the oppressor, is a traitor to his profession. He has ceased to be a scholar. He is not company for clean people.   1563
—*The Man of Letters.*

Plutarch occupies a unique place in literature as an encyclopædia of Greek and Roman antiquity. Whatever is eminent in fact or in fiction, in opinion, in character, in institutions, in science,—natural, moral or metaphysical,—or in memorable sayings, drew his attention and came to his pen with more or less fulness of record.   1564
—*Plutarch.*

I find him a better teacher of rhetoric than any modern. His superstitions are poetic, aspiring, affirmative. A poet might rhyme all day with hints drawn from Plutarch, page on page.   1565
—*Plutarch.*

The most remarkable literary work of the age (Faust).   1566
—*Life and Letters in New England.*

Every immorality is a departure from nature, and is punished by natural loss and deformity.   1567
—*Life and Letters in New England.*

I honor the generous ideas of the Socialists, the magnificence of their theories and the enthusiasm with which they have been urged.   1568
—*Life and Letters in New England.*

He chose, wisely no doubt for himself, to be the bachelor of thought and Nature.   He had no talent for wealth, and knew how to be poor without the least hint of squalor or inelegance.   1569
—*On Thoreau.*

I think there never was a people so choked and stultified by forms.   We adore the forms of law, instead of making them vehicles of wisdom and justice.   1570
—*Speech on Affairs in Kansas.*

I own I have little esteem for governments.   I esteem them only good in the moment when they are established.   I set the private man first.   He only who is able to stand alone is qualified to be a citizen.   1571
—*Speech on Affairs in Kansas.*

I do not know any story so gloomy as the politics of this country for the last twenty years, centralizing ever more manifestly round one spring, and that a vast crime, and ever more plainly, until it is notorious that all promotion, power and policy are dictated from one source,—illustrating the fatal effects of a false position to demoralize legislation and put the best people always at a disadvantage;—one crime always present (slavery), always to be varnished over, to find fine names for; and we free statesmen, as accomplices to the guilt, ever in the power of the grand offender.   1572
—*Speech on Affairs in Kansas.*

The old religions have a charm for most minds which it
is a little uncanny to disturb.   1573
                         —*On Theodore Parker.*

The vice charged against America is the want of sincerity
in leading men.   1574
                         —*On Theodore Parker.*

He never kept back the truth for fear to make an enemy.
** It was complained that he was bitter and harsh, that his
zeal burned with too hot a flame. ** He insisted beyond all
men in pulpits ** that the essence of Christianity is its practical morals; it is there for use, or it is nothing.   1575
                         —*On Theodore Parker.*

The brave know the brave. Fops, whether in hotels or
churches, will utter the fop's opinion.   1576
                         —*On Theodore Parker.*

He had a vast good nature, which made him tolerant and
accessible to all; fair-minded, leaning to the claim of the peti-
tioner; affable, and not sensible to the affliction which the
innumerable visits paid to him when President would have
brought to any one else.   1577
                         —*Of Abraham Lincoln.*

His heart was as great as the world, but there was no room
in it to hold the memory of a wrong.   1578
                         —*Of Lincoln, Greatness.*

His occupying the chair of state was a triumph of the good sense of mankind, and of the public conscience. This middle-class country had got a middle-class president, at last. Yes, in manners and sympathies, but not in powers, for his powers were superior. This man grew according to the need. His mind mastered the problem of the day; and as the problem grew, so did his comprehension of it. Rarely was man so fitted to the event. In the midst of fears and jealousies, in the Babel of counsels and parties, this man wrought incessantly with all his might and all his honesty, laboring to find what the people wanted, and how to obtain that. It cannot be said there is any exaggeration of his worth. If ever a man was fairly tested, he was. There was no lack of resistance, nor of slander, nor of ridicule.   1579
—Of Abraham Lincoln.

This country does not lie here in the sun causeless; and though it may not be easy to define its influence, men feel already its emancipating quality in the careless self-reliance of the manners, in the freedom of thought, in the direct roads by which grievances are reached and redressed, and even in the reckless and sinister politics, not less than in purer expressions. Bad as it is, this freedom leads onward and upward,—to a Columbia of thought and art, which is the last and endless end of Columbus's adventure.   1580
—Editors' Address—1847.

I have heard that when we pronounce the name of man, we pronounce the belief of immortality. All great natures delight in stability; all great men find eternity affirmed in the promise of their faculties.   1581
—Consecration of Sleepy Hollow Cemetery.

Life is not long enough for art, nor long enough for friendship. The evidence from intellect is as valid as the evidence from love. The being that can share a thought and feeling

so sublime as confidence in truth is no mushroom. Our dis-
satisfaction with any other solution is the blazing evidence
of immortality.   1582
                    —*Consecration of Sleepy Hollow Cemetery.*

Genius is the consoler of our mortal condition, and
Shakespeare taught us that the little world of the heart is
vaster, deeper and richer than the spaces of astronomy.   1583
                    —*Shakespeare.   Second Lecture.*

He was properly a man of the world; you could not lose
him; you could not detain him; you could not disappoint
him, for at any point on land or sea he found the objects
of his researches. *** He belonged to that wonderful German
nation, the foremost scholars in all history.   1584
                    —*Of Humboldt.*

One wonders sometimes that the churches still retain so many
votaries, when he reads the histories of the Church.   There
is an element of childish infatuation in them which does not
exalt our respect for man.   Read in Michelet, that in Europe,
for twelve or fourteen centuries, God the Father had no temple
and no altar.   The Holy Ghost and the Son of Mary were
worshipped, and in the thirteenth century the First Person
began to appear at the side of his Son, in pictures and in
sculpture, for worship, but only through favor of his Son.
These mortifying puerilities abound in religious history.   But
as soon as every man is apprised of the Divine Presence within
his own mind,—is apprised that the perfect law of duty corresponds with the laws of chemistry, of vegetation, of astronomy, as face to face in a glass; that the basis of duty, the order
of society, the power of character, the wealth of culture, the
perfection of taste, all draw their essence from this moral sentiment, then we have a religion that exalts, that commands all
the social and all the private action.   1585
                    —*Remarks at Religious Asso. 1867.*

The Author of Nature has not left himself without a witness in any sane mind; that the moral sentiment speaks to every man the law after which the Universe was made; that we find parity, identity of design, through Nature, and benefit to be the uniform aim; that there is a force always at work to make the best better and the worst good.   1586
—*Remarks at Religious Asso. 1869.*

I am glad to believe society contains a class of humble souls who enjoy the luxury of a religion that does not degrade; who think it the highest worship to expect of Heaven the most and the best; who do not wonder that there was a Christ, but that there were not a thousand; who have conceived an infinite hope for mankind; who believe that the history of Jesus is the history of every man, written large.   1587
—*Remarks at Religious Asso. 1869.*

In books I have the history or the energy of the past. Angels they are to us of entertainment, sympathy and provocation. With them many of us spend the most of our life,—these silent guides,—these tractable prophets, historians, and singers, whose embalmed life is the highest feat of art; who now cast their moonlight illumination over solitude, weariness and fallen fortunes.   1588
—*Address, Concord Library.*

If a man can make a better mouse-trap than his neighbor, though he build his house in the woods, the world will make a beaten path to his door.*   1589
—*Attributed to Emerson (?).*

The memory plays a great part in settling the intellectual rank of men. We estimate a man by how much he remembers.   1590
—*Of Memory.*

---

*(In substance: In Nature, Chap., Commodity, p. 14, 1836; Journal, 1855; Borrowings, by Sarah B. Yule, 1889.)

Some days are bright with thought and sentiment, and we live a year in a day. *** I would rather have a perfect recollection of all I have thought and felt in a day or a week of high activity than read all the books that have been published in a century.   1591
                                                      —*Of Memory.*

Nature kills egotism and conceit; deals strictly with us; and gives sanity; so that it was the practice of the Orientals, to let insane persons wander at their own will.   1592
                                                      —*On Country Life.*

But there are more insane persons than are called so, or are under treatment in hospitals.   The crowd in the cities, at the hotels, theatres, card-tables, the speculators **** are all more or less mad.   1593
                                                      —*On Country Life.*

But in all works of human art there is deduction to be made for blunder and falsehood.   1594
                                                      —*On Country Life.*

Every new perception of the method and beauty of Nature gives a new shock of surprise and pleasure.   1595
                                                      —*On Country Life.*

Give me a climate where people think well and construct well,—I will spend six months there, and you may have all the rest of my years.   1596
                                                      —*Of Boston.*

It is the property of the religious sentiment to be the most refining of all influences.   No external advantages, no good birth or breeding, no culture of the taste, no habit of command, no association with the elegant,—even no depth of affection that does not rise to a religious sentiment, can bestow that delicacy and grandeur of bearing which belong only to a mind accustomed to celestial conversation.   All else is coarse and external; all else is tailoring and cosmetics beside this.   1597

—*Of Boston.*

Nature is a frugal mother and never gives without measure. When she has work to do, she qualifies men for that and sends them equipped for that.   1598

—*Of Boston.*

It is almost a proverb that a great man has not a great son.
                                                     1599
—*Of Boston.*

There is something pleasing in the affection with which we can regard a man who died a hundred and sixty years ago in the other hemisphere, who, in respect to personal relations, is to us as the wind, yet by an influence purely spiritual makes us jealous for his fame as for that of a near friend.   He is identified in the mind with all select and holy images, with the supreme interests of the human race.   1600

—*On Milton.*

The most devout man of his time, he frequented no church; probably from a disgust at the fierce spirit of the pulpits.   And so, throughout all his actions and opinions, is he a consistent spiritualist, or believer in the omnipotence of spiritual laws. He wished that his writings should be communicated only to those who desired to see them.   He thought nothing honest was low.   He thought he could be famous only in proportion as he enjoyed the approbation of the good.   1601

—*On Milton.*

Literature is but a poor trick, you will say, when it busies itself to make words pass for things.   1602
—On Art and Criticism.

Speak with the vulgar, think with the wise.   1603
—On Art and Criticism.

The Devil in philosophy is absolute negation, falsehood, nothing; and in the popular mind, the Devil is a malignant person.   1604
—On Art and Criticism.

What the poet omits exalts every syllable that he writes.
1605
—On Art and Criticism.

Shakespeare is nothing but a large utterance. We cannot find that anything in his age was more worth expression than anything in ours; nor give any account of his existence, but only the fact that there was a wonderful symbolizer and expressor, who has no rival in all ages and who has thrown an accidental lustre over his time and subject.   1606
—On Art and Criticism.

The art of writing is the highest of those permitted to man as drawing directly from the soul, and the means or material it uses are also of soul. It brings man into alliance with what is great and eternal. It discloses to him the variety and splendor of his resources. And there is much in literature that draws us with a sublime charm—the superincumbent necessity by which each writer, an infirm, capricious, fragmentary soul, is made to utter his part in the chorus of humanity, is enriched by thoughts which flow from all past minds, shares the hope of all existing minds; so that, whilst the world is made of youthful, helpless children of a day, literature resounds with the music of united vast ideas of affirmation and of moral truth.   1607
—On Art and Criticism.

EPIGRAMS*

Blame is safer than praise.   1608

Every reform was once a private opinion.   1609

Life is a boundless privilege.   1610

The lesson conveyed is Be, not Seem.   1611

The joy of the spirit indicates its strength.   1612

Manners are the happy way of doing things.   1613

Every artist was once an amateur.   1614

We acquire the strength we have overcome.   1615

Nothing great was ever achieved without enthusiasm.   1616

My life is for itself, and not for a spectacle.   1617

The borrower runs in his own debt.   1618

For every benefit you receive a tax is levied.   1619

Prudence is the virtue of the senses.   1620

A little integrity is better than any career.   1621

Self-trust is the first secret of success.   1622

Never was a sincere word utterly lost.   1623

Entire self-reliance belongs to the intellect.   1624

*These Epigrams, with many others found in this volume, are also published in small pocket-edition under the title, "Philosograms of Emerson".

Inspiration makes solitude anywhere.   1625

The first lesson of history is the good of evil.   1626

Life is a succession of lessons which must be lived to be
understood.   1627

We must learn by laughter as well as by tears and
terrors.   1628

Health is a condition of wisdom, and the sign of cheerfulness.   1629

Genius and virtue, like diamonds, are best plain set.   1630

Wit makes its own welcome and levels all distinctions. 1631

Success treads on every right step.   1632

Every day is Doomsday.   1633

Better be a nettle in the side of your friends than his
echo.   1634

A man's friends are his magnetisms.   1635

Friends such as we desire are dreams and fables.   1636

Make yourself necessary to somebody.   1637

A friend is the hope of the heart.   1638

Whoso would be a man must be a non-conformist.   1639

No man had ever a defect that was not somewhere made

useful to him.   1640

Every man in his life time needs to thank his faults. 1641

Our strength grows out of our weakness. 1642

A great man is always willing to be little. 1643

Man's life is a progress, not a station. 1644

Every great man is a unique. 1645

Man is a stream whose source is hidden. 1646

The key to every man is his thought. 1647

The man is only half himself; the other half is his expression. 1648

We believe in ourselves as we do not believe in others. 1649

Personal force never goes out of fashion. 1650

The only gift is a portion of thyself. 1651

No man is quite sane,—each has a vein of folly in his composition. 1652

Every man is a channel through which heaven floweth. 1653

Great men exist that there may be greater men. 1654

Every man has a history worth knowing, if he could tell it. 1655

All healthy things are sweet-tempered. 1656

The best things are of secular growth. 1657

Moral qualities rule the world.   1658

One may be too punctual and too precise.   1659

Let us not be the victims of words.   1660

The law is only a memorandum   1661

Every hero becomes a bore at last.   1662

The force of character is cumulative.   1663

Character is higher than intellect.   1664

Character teaches over our head.   1665

To be great is to be misunderstood.   1666

The virtues are economists, but some of the vices are
also.   1667

Character and wit have their own magnetism.   ·   1668

A public oration is an escapade, an apology, not a
speech, not a man.   1669

Activity is contagious.   1670

Without the rich heart wealth is an ugly beggar.   1671

He only is rich who owns the day.   1672

He is great who confers the most benefits.   1673

Self-respect is the early form in which greatness appears.
                                                                   1674

·

Our spontaneous action is always the best.   1675

A strenuous soul hates cheap successes.   1676

Do your work and I shall know you.   1677

There is no calamity which right words will not begin
to redress.   1678

If you would liberate me you must be free.   1679

The cheapness of man is every day's tragedy.   1680

A man must thank his defects, and stand in some terror
of his talents.   1681

A man is the prisoner of his power.   1682

Self-reliance is the basis of behaviour.   1683

Every man's task is his life-preserver.   1684

All great men come out of the middle classes.   1685

Every man is entitled to be valued by his best moment.   1686

Men are ennobled by morals and by intellect.   1687

A man is a god in ruins.   1688

He who does a good deed is instantly ennobled.   1689

All men are poets at heart.   1690

Character is Nature in the highest form.   1691

Our life is March weather, savage and serene in one hour.   1692

All things are engaged in writing their history.   1693

Nature turns all malfeasance to good.   1694

Nature is a fable whose moral blazes through it.   1695

Nature is made to conspire with spirit to emancipate us.   1696

We are as much strangers in Nature, as we are aliens from God.   1697

What your heart thinks great is great.   The soul's emphasis is always right.   1698

Nothing can bring you peace but yourself.   1699

Nothing can bring you peace but the triumph of principles.   1700

Proverbs are the sanctuary of the intuitions.   1701

Genius is always ascetic, and piety and love.   1702

Life is a festival only to the wise.   1703

Our faith comes in moments, our vice is habitual.   1704

No facts are to me sacred; none are profane.   1705

God enters by a private door into every individual.   1706

Divinity is behind our failures, and follies also.   1707

The universe is the bride of the soul.   1708

All private sympathy is partial. 1709

Everything good in man leans on what is higher. 1710

Mankind divides itself into two classes,—benefactors and malefactors. 1711

The narrow sectarian cannot read astronomy with impunity. 1712

Language is fossil poetry. 1713

There is an optical illusion about every person we meet. 1714

All conversation is a magnetic experiment. 1715

Hitch your wagon to a star. 1716

Air is matter subdued by heat. 1717

I prize the mechanics of conversation. 'Tis pulley and lever and screw. 1718

Art actualizes thought. 1719

Art is a jealous mistress. 1720

The greatest genius is the most indebted man. 1721

You cannot see the mountain near. 1722

The originals are not original. 1723

The world exists for thought. 1724

Literature idealizes action. 1725

If I know your sect I anticipate your argument. 1726

All men in the abstract are just and good. 1727

There is always room for a man of force, and he makes room for many. 1728

A man's fortunes are the fruit of his character. 1729

Wherever there is power there is age. 1730

Every chair should be a throne and hold a king. 1731

Sensible men are very rare. 1732

Love, and you shall be loved. 1733

As we are, so we associate. 1734

Sport is the bloom and glow of perfect health. 1735

We thrive by our casualties. 1736

Everything good is on the highway. 1737

Serving others is serving us. 1738

Every advantage has its tax. 1739

Real service will not lose its nobleness. 1740

A cheerful, intelligent face is the end of culture. 1741

The times are the masquerade of the eternities.   1742

First or last you must pay your entire debt.   1743

The wise through excess of wisdom is made a fool.   1744

Every writer is a skater, and must go partly where he would, and partly where the skates carry him.

1745

KEY-WORD CONCORDANCE

MORE TITLES FROM THE BOOK TREE 1-800-700-TREE

Of Heaven and Earth: Essays Presented at the First Sitchin Studies Day, edited by Zecharia Sitchin. ISBN 1-885395-17-5 • 164 pages • 5 1/2 x 8 1/2 • trade paper • illustrated • $14.95

God Games: What Do You Do Forever?, by Neil Freer. ISBN 1-885395-39-6 • 312 pages • 6 x 9 • trade paper • $19.95

Space Travelers and the Genesis of the Human Form: Evidence of Intelligent Contact in the Solar System, by Joan d'Arc. ISBN 1-58509-127-8 • 208 pages • 6 x 9 • trade paper • illustrated • $18.95

Humanity's Extraterrestrial Origins: ET Influences on Humankind's Biological and Cultural Evolution, by Dr. Arthur David Horn with Lynette Mallory-Horn. ISBN 3-931652-31-9 • 373 pages • 6 x 9 • trade paper • $17.00

Past Shock: The Origin of Religion and Its Impact on the Human Soul, by Jack Barranger. ISBN 1-885395-08-6 • 126 pages • 6 x 9 • trade paper • illustrated • $12.95

Flying Serpents and Dragons: The Story of Mankind's Reptilian Past, by R.A. Boulay. ISBN 1-885395-38-8 • 276 pages • 6 x 9 • trade paper • illustrated • $19.95

Triumph of the Human Spirit: The Greatest Achievements of the Human Soul and How Its Power Can Change Your Life, by Paul Tice. ISBN 1-885395-57-4 • 295 pages • 6 x 9 • trade paper • illustrated • $19.95

Mysteries Explored: The Search for Human Origins, UFOs, and Religious Beginnings, by Jack Barranger and Paul Tice. ISBN 1-58509-101-4 • 104 pages • 6 x 9 • trade paper • $12.95

Mushrooms and Mankind: The Impact of Mushrooms on Human Consciousness and Religion, by James Arthur. ISBN 1-58509-151-0 • 103 pages • 6 x 9 • trade paper • $12.95

Vril or Vital Magnetism, with an Introduction by Paul Tice. ISBN 1-58509-030-1 • 124 pages • 5 1/2 x 8 1/2 • trade paper • $12.95

The Odic Force: Letters on Od and Magnetism, by Karl von Reichenbach. ISBN 1-58509-001-8 • 192 pages • 6 x 9 • trade paper • $15.95

The New Revelation: The Coming of a New Spiritual Paradigm, by Arthur Conan Doyle. ISBN 1-58509-220-7 • 124 pages • 6 x 9 • trade paper • $12.95

The Astral World: Its Scenes, Dwellers, and Phenomena, by Swami Panchadasi. ISBN 1-58509-071-9 • 104 pages • 6 x 9 • trade paper • $11.95

Reason and Belief: The Impact of Scientific Discovery on Religious and Spiritual Faith, by Sir Oliver Lodge. ISBN 1-58509-226-6 • 180 pages • 6 x 9 • trade paper • $17.95

William Blake: A Biography, by Basil De Selincourt. ISBN 1-58509-225-8 • 384 pages • 6 x 9 • trade paper • $28.95

The Divine Pymander: And Other Writings of Hermes Trismegistus, translated by John D. Chambers. ISBN 1-58509-046-8 • 196 pages • 6 x 9 • trade paper • $16.95

Theosophy and The Secret Doctrine, by Harriet L. Henderson. Includes *H.P. Blavatsky: An Outline of Her Life,* by Herbert Whyte, ISBN 1-58509-075-1 • 132 pages • 6 x 9 • trade paper • $13.95

The Light of Egypt, Volume One: The Science of the Soul and the Stars, by Thomas H. Burgoyne. ISBN 1-58509-051-4 • 320 pages • 6 x 9 • trade paper • illustrated • $24.95

The Light of Egypt, Volume Two: The Science of the Soul and the Stars, by Thomas H. Burgoyne. ISBN 1-58509-052-2 • 224 pages • 6 x 9 • trade paper • illustrated • $17.95

The Jumping Frog and 18 Other Stories: 19 Unforgettable Mark Twain Stories, by Mark Twain. ISBN 1-58509-200-2 • 128 pages • 6 x 9 • trade paper • $12.95

The Devil's Dictionary: A Guidebook for Cynics, by Ambrose Bierce. ISBN 1-58509-016-6 • 144 pages • 6 x 9 • trade paper • $12.95

The Smoky God: Or The Voyage to the Inner World, by Willis George Emerson. ISBN 1-58509-067-0 • 184 pages • 6 x 9 • trade paper • illustrated • $15.95

A Short History of the World, by H.G. Wells. ISBN 1-58509-211-8 • 320 pages • 6 x 9 • trade paper • $24.95

The Voyages and Discoveries of the Companions of Columbus, by Washington Irving. ISBN 1-58509-500-1 • 352 pages • 6 x 9 • hard cover • $39.95

History of Baalbek, by Michel Alouf. ISBN 1-58509-063-8 • 196 pages • 5 x 8 • trade paper • illustrated • $15.95

Ancient Egyptian Masonry: The Building Craft, by Sommers Clarke and R. Engelback. ISBN 1-58509-059-X • 350 pages • 6 x 9 • trade paper • illustrated • $26.95

That Old Time Religion: The Story of Religious Foundations, by Jordan Maxwell and Paul Tice. ISBN 1-58509-100-6 • 103 pages • 6 x 9 • trade paper • $12.95

The Book of Enoch: A Work of Visionary Revelation and Prophecy, Revealing Divine Secrets and Fantastic Information about Creation, Salvation, Heaven and Hell, translated by R. H. Charles. ISBN 1-58509-019-0 • 152 pages • 5 1/2 x 8 1/2 • trade paper • $13.95

The Book of Enoch: Translated from the Editor's Ethiopic Text and Edited with an Enlarged Introduction, Notes and Indexes, Together with a Reprint of the Greek Fragments, edited by R. H. Charles. ISBN 1-58509-080-8 • 448 pages • 6 x 9 • trade paper • $34.95

The Book of the Secrets of Enoch, translated from the Slavonic by W. R. Mortill. Edited, with Introduction and Notes by R. H. Charles. ISBN 1-58509-020-4 • 148 pages • 5 1/2 x 8 1/2 • trade paper • $13.95

Enuma Elish: The Seven Tablets of Creation, Volume One, by L. W. King. ISBN 1-58509-041-7 • 236 pages • 6 x 9 • trade paper • illustrated • $18.95

Enuma Elish: The Seven Tablets of Creation, Volume Two, by L. W. King. ISBN 1-58509-042-5 • 260 pages • 6 x 9 • trade paper • illustrated • $19.95

Enuma Elish, Volumes One and Two: The Seven Tablets of Creation, by L. W. King. Two volumes from above bound as one. ISBN 1-58509-043-3 • 496 pages • 6 x 9 • trade paper • illustrated • $38.90

The Archko Volume: Documents that Claim Proof to the Life, Death, and Resurrection of Christ, by Drs. McIntosh and Twyman. ISBN 1-58509-082-4 • 248 pages • 6 x 9 • trade paper • $20.95

The Lost Language of Symbolism: An Inquiry into the Origin of Certain Letters, Words, Names, Fairy-Tales, Folklore, and Mythologies, by Harold Bayley. ISBN 1-58509-070-0 • 384 pages • 6 x 9 • trade paper • $27.95

The Book of Jasher: A Suppressed Book that was Removed from the Bible, Referred to in Joshua and Second Samuel, translated by Albinus Alcuin (800 AD). ISBN 1-58509-081-6 • 304 pages • 6 x 9 • trade paper • $24.95

The Bible's Most Embarrassing Moments, with an Introduction by Paul Tice. ISBN 1-58509-025-5 • 172 pages • 5 x 8 • trade paper • $14.95

History of the Cross: The Pagan Origin and Idolatrous Adoption and Worship of the Image, by Henry Dana Ward. ISBN 1-58509-056-5 • 104 pages • 6 x 9 • trade paper • illustrated • $11.95

Was Jesus Influenced by Buddhism? A Comparative Study of the Lives and Thoughts of Gautama and Jesus, by Dwight Goddard. ISBN 1-58509-027-1 • 252 pages • 6 x 9 • trade paper • $19.95

History of the Christian Religion to the Year Two Hundred, by Charles B. Waite. ISBN 1-885395-15-9 • 556 pages. • 6 x 9 • hard cover • $25.00

Symbols, Sex, and the Stars, by Ernest Busenbark. ISBN 1-885395-19-1 • 396 pages • 5 1/2 x 8 1/2 • trade paper • $22.95

History of the First Council of Nice: A World's Christian Convention, A.D. 325, by Dean Dudley. ISBN 1-58509-023-9 • 132 pages • 5 1/2 x 8 1/2 • trade paper • $12.95

The World's Sixteen Crucified Saviors, by Kersey Graves. ISBN 1-58509-018-2 • 436 pages • 5 1/2 x 8 1/2 • trade paper • $29.95

ALSO AVAILABLE FROM THE BOOK TREE

AS A MAN THINKETH, by James Allen, $9.95
THE PATH OF PROSPERITY, by James Allen, $12.95
HOW TO DEVELOP PERSONAL MAGNETISM AND HEALING POWERS, by Anonymous, $12.95
YOUR MIND CAN HEAL YOU, by Frederick Bailes, $19.95
THOUGHT POWER: Its Control and Culture, by Annie Besant, $13.95
COSMIC CONSCIOUSNESS, by Richard Maurice Bucke, $26.95
MAGIC AND MYSTERY IN TIBET, by Alexandra David-Neel, $26.95
SPIRITUAL REALIZATIONS, by Florence Willard Day, $12.95
THE ART AND SCIENCE OF PERSONAL MAGNETISM, by Theron Dumont, $19.95
PROSPERITY, by Charles Fillmore, $18.95
THE MASTER KEY, by Charles Haanel, unabridged version, $34.95
MENTAL CHEMISTRY, by Charles Haanel, $26.95
THINK AND GROW RICH, by Napoleon Hill, $18.95
ZENTREPRENEURISM: A 21st Century Guide to the New World of Business, by Allan Holender, $19.95
CREATIVE MIND, by Ernest Holmes, $10.95
CREATIVE MIND AND SUCCESS, by Ernest Holmes, $12.95
THE GREAT SECRET, by Maurice Maeterlinck, $22.95
THE LIFE AND THE WAY, by A. K. Mozumdar, $13.95
TERTIUM ORGANUM, by P. D. Ouspensky, $26.95
THE HUMAN AURA, by Swami Panchadasi, $10.95
CONSCIOUSLY CREATING CIRCUMSTANCES, by G. W. Plummer, $12.95
THE ETHERIC DOUBLE, by A. E. Powell, $14.95
SCIENCE OF BREATH, by Yogi Ramacharaka, $11.95
THE SECRET DOOR TO SUCCESS, by Florence Scovel Shinn $12.95
THE KYBALION, by Three Initiates, $17.95
VRIL OR VITAL MAGNETISM, Introduction by Paul Tice, $12.95
IN TUNE WITH THE INFINITE, by Ralph Waldo Trine, $17.95
CREATIVE PROCESS IN THE INDIVIDUAL, by Thomas Troward, $16.95
DORE LECTURES ON MENTAL SCIENCE, by Thomas Troward, $12.95
THE EDINBURGH LECTURES, by Thomas Troward, $13.95
THE HIDDEN POWER, by Thomas Troward, $18.95
THE CLOUD UPON THE SANCTUARY, by von Eckartshausen, $12.95
THE ODIC FORCE: Letters on Od and Magnetism, by von Reichenback, $15.95
THE SCIENCE OF GETTING RICH, by Wallace D. Wattles, $14.95
THE ESSAYS OF SIR FRANCIS BACON, by Francis Bacon, $17.95
PERPETUAL PEACE, by Immanuel Kant, $10.95
HOW WE THINK, by John Dewey, $19.95
AFTER LIFE, WHAT? by Robert Pinansky, $12.95

Plus many more intersting titles. We pride ourselves in customer service.

TO ORDER PLEASE VISIT www.thebooktree.com OR CALL
1-800-700-TREE (8733) 24 hrs.